ENCYCLOPEDIA

of

Ad-Libs, Crazy Jokes, Insults and Wisecracks

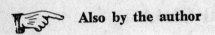 **Also by the author**

5,000 One and Two Liners for Any and Every Occasion, Parker, 1973

ENCYCLOPEDIA

of

Ad-Libs, Crazy Jokes, Insults and Wisecracks

Leopold Fechtner

Parker Publishing Company, Inc., West Nyack, New York

Library of Congress Cataloging in Publication Data

Fechtner, Leopold
    Encyclopedia of ad-libs, crazy jokes, insults,
and wisecracks.

    1. American wit and humor. I. Title.
PN6162.F37   817'.008   76-43358
ISBN 0-13-275255-7

*This book is dedicated to all my friends who
helped me with advice and material...*

*...and to my lovely wife, Fini
who claims I'm the funniest man she ever met.*

What This Book Will Do for You

While this book will definitely amuse you, more importantly it will serve you as an invaluable aid in your business and personal life.

Regardless of your business, you are in constant contact with others—superiors, fellow workers, customers, clients, competitors—and the ability to easily inject humor into your conversations is a valuable attribute. Imagine how confident you would feel if you had tested, humorous material at your fingertips for almost any occasion and on almost any topic.

In addition, everyone is occasionally called upon to address a group, be it business, civic or social. Now, you can add sparkle to your remarks by including a few humorous items that will break the ice and guarantee that your talk will go smoothly.

Here is a new type of humor book. Its purpose is to provide you with a large variety of the best humorous material available to help you make your conversations and speeches more interesting and entertaining.

This is a book that anyone can use successfully since it offers a rich selection of the latest ad-libs, gags, wisecracks and quips. Here is a fresh approach to the best of American humor—unusual, entertaining, compact, witty, alive and funny.

This stimulating guidebook is divided into five parts by type of humor. Within each part, there are topics organized alphabetically to enable you to easily find the material you want to use. Then, within each topic, the material is also in alphabetical order.

Whether you are preparing a speech, want some funny material for your friendly gatherings, or just wish to interject some humor into your daily conversations, you can choose from more than 5,000 items. This ensures that you will always be selecting fresh material to amuse your associates and friends.

Every morning pick a few items at random, remember them, and tell them to your friends and neighbors. Try putting them into your own words, mix them, change them and work on them. You'll be surprised to see how easy it is to really amuse people with this good, fresh material. People like to be amused and entertained and, with the help of this book, you will have the ability to do just that.

This book, a handy reference tool, will help you supply the right joke or pun, whether you wish to illustrate a point, enliven a speech, or pep up your daily conversation.

The material is broad in scope, ranging from the ageless husband and wife jokes to contemporary material on inflation and pollution. Examine this fascinating material and see how it can add punch to your speeches. Browse through this stockpile of wit, use some in your next conversation and get a rewarding sense of satisfaction from seeing people smile.

I have carefully handpicked this material from the two million funny items in my personal Humor Library and sincerely believe that this unique collection will prove to be extremely useful, as well as highly entertaining.

Leopold Fechtner

Kew Gardens, N.Y.

CONTENTS

Part 1 Ad-Libs (con't)

Part 1 Ad-Libs (con't)

ENCYCLOPEDIA

of

Ad-Libs, Crazy Jokes, Insults and Wisecracks

1

Ad-Libs

Adam and Eve

Adam and Eve were the first pair who ate the first apple.

Adam was the first radio fan to construct a loud speaker out of his spare parts.

Adam had no mother-in-law—that's why he lived in paradise.

Adam never had to listen to Eve tell about the other men she could have married.

As Adam said in the Garden of Eden, "Who is going to know?"

Eve was the first chicken that ever ruined a man's garden.

Eve was the first person who ate herself out of house and home.

When Eve asked Adam, "Do you love me?" he replied, "Who else?"

The trouble in the Garden of Eden wasn't caused by an apple—but by a green pair.

It was an apple that made Adam tell, and it was an apple that made William Tell.

It wasn't the apple on the tree that caused all the trouble—it was the peach on the ground.

The only man who ever enjoyed falling leaves was Adam.

Remember when Eve said to Adam, "I think I'll turn over a new leaf!"

Adam's first day was very long because there was no Eve.

Advice

Advice to all young men: the stork is the bird with the largest bill.

When good advice goes in one ear and out the other, it leaves a vacuum in between.

The best cure for snoring is to develop insomnia.

The best place to look for a helping hand is at the end of your own arm.

To keep snow from sticking to your snow shovel, move to Florida.

When in charge: ponder. When in trouble: delegate. When in doubt: mumble!

Be nice to people until you make a million dollars; then people will be nice to you.

The trouble with good advice is that is usually interferes with your plans.

It's better to be over the hill than under it.

In an underdeveloped country, don't drink the water. In a developed country, don't breathe.

Gargling the first thing in the morning is a good way to find out if your neck leaks.

I almost drowned last night. Please—never take acupuncture on a waterbed.

You don't have to wear a T-shirt while serving tea.

Age

Age is something that makes wine worth more and people worth less.

Age is mostly a matter of mind. If you don't mind it, it doesn't matter.

Age is something a woman conceals because a man usually never acts his.

Ask any woman her age and nine out of ten will guess wrong.

It's always tough to tell a woman's age—at least for her.

Her real age is the only secret a woman would keep.

You should never trust a woman who tells her real age—a woman who would tell that, would tell anything.

If you really want to learn a woman's true age, ask somebody who doesn't like her.

We are living today in the age of plenty: plenty problems, plenty bills, plenty troubles.

Forty was the most difficult age for her to pass—it took her eight years.

Twenty years from now the modern girl will be five years older.

Growing old isn't so bad when you consider the alternative.

Why is it that a person your own age always looks older than you?

Today a girl has a hard time trying to look as young as her mother.

At my age all women look alike: Good!

At last she admitted she was forty! But she didn't say when.

The three ages of men: underage, overage and average.

I really don't know much about growing old. After all, I never did it before.

This is the age of tension. Everybody lives in the fear of bending, breaking or mutilating an IBM card.

You will always stay young if you live honestly, eat slowly, worship faithfully, and lie about your age.

Alaska

Alaska is great if you happen to be a polar bear.

Alaska is the state where you think of Canada as the tropics.

You can tell when it's summer in Alaska—the snow is wetter.

Anniversary

Last week my wife and I celebrated our tin anniversary—12 years of eating TV Dinners.

Anniversaries are like martinis: After a few you don't bother to count them.

Today I'm celebrating an anniversary—I've been broke for seven years.

Apartment

I live in a small, modern apartment. So I have very little room to complain.

My landlord is very considerate. He gives you plenty of heat in July, even if you don't ask for it.

In our apartment we have a kitchen area, a sleeping area and a bathroom area—all in the same area.

My apartment is antique and so is my wife.

There are three kinds of apartment buildings in New York today: they're either going UP, coming DOWN or fully RENTED.

The walls in my apartment are so thin that I can hear the people next door complaining about the thin walls.

My apartment is usually so cold that the lights go on when I open the door.

The floor is so thin, my wife scrubbed the floor once and fell through to the basement.

Cold? The only thing that isn't frozen is the rent.

Aviation

This airline is so cheap, instead of showing movies they show snapshots of the pilots.

This airline is so small, you have to have the exact change to get on the plane.

This airline will go a long way toward bringing back rail travel.

This airline is so eager to please you, if they don't have what you want, they'll send it to you airmail.

This airline was so run down, even the pilot took out flight insurance.

This airline was so poor, while they showed movies the pilot came around selling popcorn.

This airline was so poor, to entertain the passengers the stewardess told jokes.

This airline was so poor, they had to merge with another airline. To bad they merged in mid-air.

This airline is so poor, they showed coming attractions of movies that would be shown on other airlines.

This airline is so poor, they show slides instead of movies.

This airline is so poor, instead of showing movies the pilot buzzes drive-in movies.

I wouldn't fly this airline if it were the only one in the country and we had to evacuate because of a national emergency.

I wonder why our pilot just jumped out the window with his parachute. Maybe we're in trouble and he went out to get help.

On this plane they show silent films so they won't disturb the sleeping passengers.

Jet travel lets us see less and less of more and more. Faster and faster.

Some airlines would do anything to entertain their passengers. The latest improvements are bowling alleys and ping-pong tables in the plane.

An airplane is the only place where you can't walk out on a dull movie.

Our skies are so crowded now that every cloud has a silver airliner.

Our plane circled the airport so long, it wore a big hole in one of the air pockets.

A friend of mine got on a plane in New York at 9 pm and arrived in Paris 7 hours later. Boy, was he mad! He wanted to go to Chicago.

Thanks to modern air travel we can now be sick in countries we never even knew existed before.

We had a tough flight; the plane was bouncing around all night. The only person who fell asleep was the pilot.

That's nothing—our co-pilot asked a passenger how to get to the cockpit.

The jets are so fast nowadays, it's possible to have breakfast in New York and then arrive in Los Angeles to find nobody awake yet.

Since all airlines show movies now, the stewardesses ask, "Coffee, tea, or popcorn?"

I refuse to fly. I have a terrible fear of movies.

It costs less and less each year to fly to Europe, and more and more to get to the airport.

He claims he visited three countries while his luggage had visited five.

What bothers me is—if those space scientists are so smart, why do they count backwards?

This airline is so cheap, all passengers have to chip in to buy gas.

Babies

I was a war baby. My parents took a look at me and started fighting.

I didn't even look at our baby until he was two years old. Let's face it—if you've seen one, you've seen them all.

My parents called me Surrender. They took one look at me and gave up.

Isn't it wonderful, doctor? Three more payments and the baby will be ours.

Smart! One hour after I was born I learned how to yawn.

I always wondered why babies suck their thumb. Then I tasted baby food.

Bank-Banking

I just read a book with nothing in it: my bankbook.

I used to be a draft clerk in a bank. I opened and shut windows.

I just bought a house. On a clear day I can see the bank that holds the mortgage.

I complimented the bank on the calendar they sent me. It's been right every month so far.

I was a director at the bank. I directed people to the safes.

I always keep money in my checking account. It's like money in the bank.

I wouldn't say my account is very low, but my bank just sent me last year's calendar.

I always take my salary to the bank. I have to—it's too small to go by itself.

I took all my money out of the bank last night. Since the bank closes at three in the afternoon, it wasn't easy.

Anybody who can afford to pay the interest these days doesn't need the loan.

Yes sir, your loan has been approved, but now you need another one to cover the interest on it.

My bank is very careful. They send out their calendar one month at a time.

My checking account balances perfectly. I'm overdrawn exactly what I'm short.

Bars

I'm watching my drinking. I only visit bars that have mirrors.

Many a man goes into a bar for an eye-opener and comes out blind.

He's leaned on so many bars, his clothes have padded elbows.

They redecorated my favorite bar. They put new drunks around it.

I go to an expensive bar. They still charge $24 for a Manhattan.

They serve a Scotch here that should be deported.

After five drinks, they play the *Star Spangled Banner* to see who can still stand up.

Bathing

Every morning I jump into a cold tub—then I fill it with hot water.

Now where is that handsome life guard? I've been yelling "help" for half an hour.

Whenever you go to a place that features sand, sun and surf, you come back burned, bushed and broke.

Bathing Suit

A modern bathing suit is two bandanas and a worried look.

A bikini is half a bathing suit that costs twice as much.

Two kinds of girls wear bikinis—those who have the figure and those who have the nerve.

Whoever designs women's bathing suits is working himself out of a job.

This year the girls are showing a lot of bathing suits, and the bathing suits are showing a lot of girls.

The modern bathing suit is not only going out of style but out of sight as well.

Birthdays

What do you give a wife who has everything and none of it is paid for?

I gave her a bridge lamp for her birthday, but she made me put it back on the bridge.

I promised her a mink for her birthday if she'd keep his cage clean.

She gave me a nice pipe for my birthday, with a stove attached to it.

I bought her an electric typewriter and now I'm looking for a chair to match.

She'd like to get a few cards for her birthday—like American Express, Diner's Club and Master Charge.

I promise her anything but she'll get nothing.

Last year I gave her a chair as a present. This year I had it wired.

I gave my son a book as a present, but he doesn't know what to do with it—there's no place to put the batteries.

Birthday Cake

Instead of candles they build a bonfire in the center of the cake.

Our air conditioner was doing fine until my wife lit the candles on her birthday cake.

Her birthday cake had 39 candles arranged in the form of a question mark.

She made me a birthday cake and put the candles inside.

Books

I read a book from cover to cover and found it very interesting—not the pages, just the covers.

There is a book out now for cannibals called, *How to Serve Your Fellow Man.*

This book was so exciting, I couldn't finish it until I put it down.

The only kinds of books I really like are checkbooks.

Business

Is he a good business man! He sold me a Christmas tree a day after Christmas.

Business is so bad, people are returning things they didn't even buy.

They now have a computer that's so human, on Monday morning it comes in ten minutes late.

They say things are looking up, and they're right. Food is up, clothing is up, taxes are up.

Ten years ago he started on a shoestring and today he has two shoestrings.

Last year I opened up a general store, but it failed. Seems nobody buys generals these days.

All day I tell people to go fly a kite—because I sell kites.

It is wise to learn a trade. Then you will always know what kind of work it is you are out of.

Doing business without advertising is like winking at a girl in the dark. *You* know what you're doing, but no one else does.

Our efficiency expert saved our company 150 dollars a week. He quit.

Say, boss, if you can't give me a raise, how about the same pay more often?

Many a going business is going the wrong way.

Everybody says business is looking up. What else can it do? It's flat on its back!

Business is so slow right now, a fellow walked into a place to change a $20 bill and they made him a partner.

One of the hardest things about business is minding your own.

Yes, that's right. I'm giving you a raise because I want your last week here to be a happy one.

Business is marvelous right now. It's fifty percent ahead of last year, but we all hope it will pick up.

The men who manufacture woolen underwear irritate a lot of people.

A hula dancer has no future. It's such a shaky business.

Is there anything so embarrassing as watching the boss doing something you told him couldn't be done?

Say, today is Monday, tomorrow will be Tuesday, and the day after Wednesday. Half of the week is gone and you didn't do a thing yet.

A big shot is a man who has his name printed on company letterheads because no one can read his signature.

This is the lowest February sales we ever had, but it's always this way before Christmas.

This year business has gone directly from the summer slump into the fall recession.

What a store! If you ask for an item below 50 dollars, they look in the waste basket.

A real executive is a man who can hand a letter back to a red-headed stenographer for the third time.

Work faithfully eight hours a day and don't worry. Then in time you will become the boss, work twelve hours a day, and do all the worrying.

Even the florist complained about the business. There was plenty of green around his shop but none of it was in the cash register.

There are two reasons why people don't mind their business: they either have no mind or they have no business.

His business is now on a solid foundation: on the rocks!

Cars

My car can pass anything on the road, providing it's going in the opposite direction.

My car couldn't go over 50 even if it were pushed.

My car has three speeds: pull, push, and neutral.

My car had a squeak in the back. It turned out to be my wife.

My car has every convenience except a push button to lower the payments.

My car has something that will last a lifetime: monthly payments.

My car has two speeds: slow and stop.

My car? I have a watch that runs better and faster.

My car is just like a baby. It won't go anywhere without a rattle.

My car is so long, I got a parking ticket in Newark and in Hoboken at the same time.

My car is so long, it takes five minutes to go through a two-minute car wash.

My car is so old, it doesn't have a clock on the dashboard. It has a sun dial.

My car is so old, the insurance covers fire, theft and Indian raids.

My car is so small, I have to go to Juvenile Court to pay my parking tickets.

My car is so small, the glove compartment holds only two fingers.

My car just came back from the auto laundry and all the buttons are missing.

My car never skids, never breaks down, never gets a flat—I only wish I could start it.

My car? Nobody can fix it, the garages won't park it, it can't be moved, I can't start it, and nobody would even steal it.

My car was being recalled to correct three missing payments.

My car works on push buttons. If the buttons don't work, you get out and push.

My tires are so thin you can almost see the air.

The trouble is that the car of tomorrow is being driven on the highway of yesterday by the driver of today.

Children

I have to go home now. If I'm not home by 10 pm, my father rents out my room.

Well, if you don't buy me some ice cream I'll call you Grandma in front of all those people!

Ma, if the Lord gives us our daily bread, and Santa brings presents, and the stork brings babies, then what's the use of having Daddy around?

Mother! There are only clean towels in the bathroom. Should I start one?

But, Ma, how can I button my dress when all the buttons are in the back and I'm in the front?

Daddy, I know matches are made in heaven but where do cigar lighters come from?

Here is my report card, Daddy, and one of yours I found in the attic.

Dad, I'm running away from home. Please call me a taxi!

Mom, why did you bring that book I didn't want to be read to out of up for?

But, Daddy, why can't I marry your mother? You married mine!

If ink is not expensive, then why did Mother get so upset when I spilled a whole bottle on the new carpet?

I don't get the best marks in school, Dad. Do you get the best salary at the office?

Now, listen, children. There will be a special prize for any child who leaves this party right now!

Now, junior, be a good boy and say "ahh" so the doctor can get his finger out of your mouth.

Junior, I'm not going to give you any more martinis if all you do is eat the olives!

Sometimes I think my parents didn't want me. When I was a baby they always put a teddy bear in my crib. A live one!

It is proven that children hold a marriage together while tearing the house apart.

I'm not worried about what modern children know—I'm just worried how they found out.

Christmas

Christmas is the time when all that matters is the presents.

Christmas is the time when you wish people didn't come in different sizes.

Christmas is the time of the year when women get santamental!

Christmas always worries me. My wife gives me presents I can't afford.

This Christmas if you really want to shake somebody up, give him a gift certificate for Forest Lawn.

At Christmas we always exchange presents. I exchange the one she gave me and she exchanges the one I gave her.

Every Christmas she hung up her stockings, but all she ever got was a run.

Why does Christmas always come when the stores are most crowded?

For Christmas I bought my son an electric train for me to play with.

By the time I found a place to park, Christmas was over.

Misery is when Christmas has come and gone, but your relatives haven't.

She doesn't want much for Christmas. Just a little radio with a Cadillac attached to it.

The first thing to turn green in the spring is Christmas jewelry.

The best Christmas cigar I ever received was the one that burned a hole in my Christmas tie.

There are two kinds of Christmas presents: those you don't like and those you don't get.

You should have seen what my child gave me last Christmas: measles!

I made a big mistake at the office Christmas party. I kissed the boss's secretary hello and my job goodbye.

Have you priced Christmas trees lately? It's the first time I had a tree trim me.

I gave her the best jewelry five dollars could buy.

Clothes

This suit was made to order, but the man didn't pick it up so I took it.

For her birthday I bought her a tight skirt with a straight jacket.

They sold me a form-fitting suit, but I don't have the form it fits.

This suit cost me a hundred dollars—just to clean!

These are my summer clothes. Summer paid for and summer not.

What the well-dressed girl will wear this year is less.

Your gown reminds me of a song: Sweet and Low.

I never wear my new shoes until I've walked in them a day or so.

My coat has only one defect. It covers my shoes.

Some of those new paper dresses cost more than 100 dollars. It's cheaper to wear the money.

Isn't that a fine suit? And so reasonable. Just two payments and a change of address.

You've heard of strapless and backless gowns? Hers was shapeless and hopeless.

My new summer suit is so cool, if I wear it all day I catch a cold.

By the time a man is successful enough to buy his wife dresses for a fancy figure, she no longer has one.

Coffee

Each morning my wife and the coffee begin to boil at the same time.

She needs a full day to make instant coffee.

I never drink coffee in the morning. It keeps me awake all day.

What this country really needs is a 9 to 5 coffee break!

My wife's coffee won't keep you awake—unless you drink it!

I do drink plenty of water, doctor, but my wife calls it coffee.

They now have a drink that's part Ovaltine and part coffee. It makes you yawn but you can't sleep.

Some people drink coffee and can't sleep. With me it's just the opposite: when I sleep I can't drink coffee.

My wife serves blended coffee—today's and yesterday's.

My father was killed by coffee. A 100 pound sack fell on his head.

My wife always serves coffee in a container. It gives her coffee a distinctive cardboard taste.

The trouble with Italian coffee is that a week later you're sleepy again.

She went blind drinking coffee. She left the spoon in the cup.

They serve real strong coffee here: one cup and you perk all night.

I bought an automatic coffee machine. But who wants to drink automatic coffee?

I often wondered why the English were tea drinkers—until I tasted their coffee.

Nowadays it isn't the caffeine that keeps you awake: it's the price of coffee that doesn't let you sleep.

Every morning I get up and make coffee in my pajamas. Some day I'll try a coffee pot.

Comedian

He couldn't get a standing ovation even if he sang the *Star-Spangled Banner.*

He is known as a character actor. When he shows any character he's acting.

He has a custom-made telephone. It doesn't ring—it applauds.

He once got a standing ovation—no chairs!

His fan club just met in a phone booth.

He is a finished comedian. Not only now, forever!

He has appeared on radio, TV, stage and screen. There's no way to escape him.

He would like to say something funny but he doesn't want to break the spell.

I would like to tell a joke but you would only laugh at me.

I know, I'm funny. When they ask me what I do, I tell them I'm a comic. It always makes them laugh.

My manager gave me a nice dressing room but it costs me a dime every time I want to get in.

A comedian is...

> ... a man who has a gift of gag.
> ... a man who originates old jokes.
> ... a man with a fun-track mind.
> ... a man who makes dough out of corn.
> ... a man who doesn't think he's funny but hopes he will be.

Cooking

Tonight we're having smorgasbord. It's in the refrigerator.

She can boil the softest hard-boiled egg you've ever seen.

Say, the flour you sold me last week was sure tough. I made some biscuits and we couldn't eat them.

A rare steak is one that costs less than $5.

Of course, you have it easy. All you have to do is prepare and cook it, while I have to eat it!

Yes, honey, it's nice and crisp, but tapioca isn't supposed to be nice and crisp.

The last soup of the day she fixed me from the soup of the month gave me indigestion for a week.

How do you want your eggs this morning? Without ham or without bacon?

Tell me, honey, what was this before you cooked it?

This submarine sandwich you made me tonight is starting to surface.

Okay, I take it back. This stringy, dry, overcooked roast beef is delicious!

I think I just broke a tooth on your gravy.

I'm not criticizing my wife's cooking, but last night she burned the potato salad.

Dancing

I stepped out on the dance floor and people made fun of me. The next time I'm gonna take a girl along.

When kids dance nowadays they don't talk, they don't touch, they don't even look at each other. Just like being married for 30 years.

This place was so old-fashioned, the couples were dancing together.

Nowadays you never know if your partner is a good dancer or if he's drunk.

I went to a square dance and really danced with a square.

The big advantage in dancing with a fat girl is that your toes are safe.

She only dances with me so she can stamp on my toes.

Dates

There are 400 beautiful girls in town and he always dates the others.

A modern mother worries when her daughter comes home early from a date.

He is a perfect gentleman, but I think it's better than no boy friend at all.

Jim and I? We're not going steady any more. I went on a blind date and there he was.

It was a real baseball romance. She had all the curves and he did all the pitching.

I'd introduce you, but she isn't the type I'd want you to know.

They met on a blind date and it ripened into friendship, then it rotted into marriage.

You remember our last date? Well, that's what it was.

I don't go out with strange men and you're one of the strangest men I've ever met.

My date was very interesting. She was so eager she wore a bridal gown.

Diet

There's no use going on a diet if you have to starve to death to live longer.

New diet food comes in cans. You open it and there's nothing in it.

No wonder she's fat. She claims eating makes her hungry.

She is allowed to eat all she wants of anything she doesn't like.

She went on a banana diet. Now she looks like one.

Here's a new diet. You can eat all you want—steaks, spaghetti, ice cream—but only with chopsticks.

As soon as she went on a diet, her stock went down and her weight went up.

Diets are for people who are thick and tired of it.

She skips breakfast and luncheon, then spends the day munchin'.

When she went on a diet, the first thing she lost was her temper.

It's not difficult to diet these days. Just eat what you can afford.

An onion builds you up physically and tears you down socially.

You can't eat your cake and diet too.

She lost ten pounds lately. She is now on a low salary diet.

The best reducing plan is to keep your mouth and the refrigerator shut.

Dieting is a trying time when you stop eating food and start eating calories.

The trouble with reducing is that it calls for less food and your appetite calls for more.

She takes her reducing pill twice a day in a chocolate malt.

She won't eat anything that starts with the letter Z.

They now have a new diet—watch your food! You don't taste it, you just watch it!

Whenever my wife goes on a new diet, all she loses is her sense of humor.

I'd go on a diet, but I happen to be a poor loser.

She now has a raw diet. She eats her breakfast raw, her lunch raw, but for dinner she puts on some clothes.

By the time you're making enough money to afford sugar, your doctor says you can't have it.

For lunch I had a large pizza with sausage, pepperoni and extra cheese. And then a diet cola.

The toughest part of dieting isn't watching what you eat; it's watching what your friends eat.

A health addict is one who eats health food so he won't ruin his health and have to eat health food.

Everything is relative: a two-week vacation never seems as long as two weeks on a diet.

The new reducing salon is called Thinner Sanctum.

The best place for the bathroom scale is in front of your refrigerator.

I bought a reducing machine. Now I'm starving to death to keep up the payments.

It took a lot of will power, but finally I gave up trying to diet.

More diets begin in dress shops than in doctor's offices.

Calories don't count—they multiply!

You should watch your diet—not eat it!

Doctor

My doctor, before treating my nose and ear, asked for an arm and a leg.

My doctor couldn't be a very good doctor. All his patients are sick.

My doctor cured me of insomnia, but still, I lie awake half the night thinking about my sleeplessness.

My doctor discovered a cure for which there is no disease.

My doctor doesn't make house calls, but if you're sick more than five days he sends you a get-well card.

My doctor finally found out what I had and relieved me of most of it.

My doctor gave me a prescription to take and believe me, it was the worst tasting paper I ever ate.

My doctor gave me six months to live, but when I told him I couldn't pay his bill, he gave me another six months.

My doctor gave me three pills. The blue one is for before dinner. The red one is for after dinner and the yellow one is dinner.

My doctor has more degrees than a thermometer.

My doctor has magic hands. Every time he touches me, $50 disappears.

My doctor has the flu. Now he's getting a taste of his own medicine.

My doctor is a man who is ready to lend you a healthy hand.

My doctor is really nice. When he treated me for double-pneumonia he sent me a bill for only one pneumonia.

My doctor just divorced his wife. Every night before going to bed she gave him an apple.

My doctor is not concerned with Medicare. He never had a patient who lived to be 65.

My doctor is so busy, sitting in his waiting room I caught three more diseases.

My doctor is so expensive, he operated on me and charged me $300 for new parts.

My doctor is so expensive, when he told me to drink lots of liquids I couldn't afford any.

My doctor is so mean. He always keeps his stethoscope in the freezer.

My doctor is so strange. When I broke my leg he taught me how to limp.

My doctor is the only man who hasn't a guaranteed cure for a cold.

My doctor ordered a change of scenery, so I moved my desk to the window.

My doctor said I needed a complete change, so I changed the doctor.

My doctor said I needed some iron in my system, so he stuck a knife in me.

My doctor said I should never sleep on an empty stomach so I always sleep on my back.

My doctor sent me a bill marked, "Long time no fee!"

My doctor sent me a get-well card and inside was a bill for 38 cents—for the card and the postage.

My doctor suggested a change of scenery so I bought some new wallpaper.

My doctor told me I'm in good shape for a man of 60. Too bad I'm only 49.

My doctor told me to eat more. Now I take three olives with my martini.

My doctor told me to give up smoking, women and liquor. Now I'm looking for another doctor.

My doctor told me to take a bath in milk. But I can't get into the bottle.

My doctor told me to take something good and warm. So I took his coat.

My doctor told me to watch my food. Where *I* eat I have to watch my *coat*.

My doctor told my wife she needs some salt air. Now every morning I fan her with a salt herring.

My doctor turned kidnapper but failed because nobody could read his ransom notes.

My doctor wanted to paint my wife's throat but she couldn't decide on the right color.

My doctor warned me to cut down on my drinking. So I switched from Four Roses to Three Feathers.

My doctor's prescription is hard to read, but his bill is nice and clear.

My doctor's reception room is always packed. I get the feeling people just come and sit until they get sick.

Drinks—Drinking

I gave up drinking. Now I have nothing to live on but food and water.

I don't spend all my money on drinks. I save some for luxuries.

He always puts a teabag in his mustache and drinks hot water.

I don't drink anything stronger than Pop. And Pop will drink anything!

Anybody who orders a soft drink has no kick coming.

Whiskey may shorten your life, but you'll see twice as much in half the time.

He drinks only to forget and the only thing he forgets is when to stop.

He is the only man who wears sunglasses to protect his eyes from the glare of his nose.

He never drinks too much, but one night he came home, opened the closet door and said, "Third floor, please!"

Does he drink? Every time he walks by a liquor store his nose lights up.

There is only one thing he won't drink: DDT.

I have read so much about the bad effect of drinking that I gave up reading.

He was trying to write a drinking song but he couldn't get past the first few bars.

When a man drinks too much he has two reasons: either he's married or he's single.

Congress is shrewd. First they put a tax on liquor. Then they raise the taxes to drive people to drink.

When I proposed a toast, my wife took some rye and gave me whole wheat.

When I don't feel well, I drink and when I drink, I don't feel well.

I was taking shots for my cold but my wife took the bottle away.

Drugstores

Aspirin is a miracle drug. A year's supply usually disappears in a month.

Expensive medicines are always good, if not for the patient at least for the druggist.

They discovered a new miracle drug. It's inexpensive—that's the miracle.

They now have a new miracle pill. You take two and you feel so bad you can't remember what ailed you in the first place.

They also sell a new cold capsule for $285—five vitamins and a ticket to Miami.

Try our new cough medicine—you'll never get any better!

Eyes

No wonder he looks so pale. All his blood is in his eyes.

Chicago is so windy, it's the only place I ever spit in my own eye.

I got my black eye because I went out looking for trouble and my eye was the first to find it.

I call my girl "Grapefruit" because every time I squeeze her she hits me in the eye.

Family

Our family has more trouble than a soap opera.

My parents called me "Surrender"—they took one look at me and gave up.

My grandfather was an old Indian fighter—because my grandmother was an old Indian.

In the middle of our living room we now have a lazy susan: my sister-in-law.

My daughter started to write poetry in the hospital. I think she took a turn for the verse.

My daughter gained 175 pounds last summer. She finally found a husband.

My child has sensitive ears. He screams every time I pull them.

She comes from such an old family, it's been condemned.

I never liked my little brother. Whenever I hit him with a hammer he would cry.

I come from a rich family. My brother is worth $50,000 dead or alive.

His monthly salary runs into three figures. His wife and two children.

She didn't come from a big family. She was sent.

It's a fine family. Mother has electricity in her hair and father has gas in his stomach.

I better go home now. I told my wife I was going out for a newspaper and that was last night.

He is so henpecked, he not only brings home the bacon, he cooks it too.

Food

He who loves rich food and cooks it, looks it.

I call our toaster "Indian" because it always sends up smoke signals.

What's wrong with frozen food? I've been eating cold dinners for years.

The hot dog nowadays has so little meat, you can eat it on Fridays.

At home I'm the boss. I always pick out the cans of food I want for supper.

For Valentine's Day my wife baked me a heart-shaped meat loaf.

To get your money nowadays you should ask for doughnuts with small holes.

Then there was the illegitimate Rice Krispie who had a snap and crackle, but no pop.

Everything is powdered now, powdered sugar, powdered coffee. Whenever I tell my wife I'm hungry, she says, "Oh, go take a powder!"

For two years she had me eating out of her hands. Then she finally bought a set of dishes.

Every morning I take a cold shower. I have grapefruit for breakfast.

Food prices are like this: if you ever catch the flu, it's cheaper to get penicillin than chicken soup.

So don't ask me what I cooked for you tonight. It's better not to know.

I don't eat eggs. I figure if the chicken doesn't want them why should I?

There is only one thing bigger than her appetite. It's her stomach!

I always eat dessert first, because life is so uncertain.

I wish her food would taste as good as it looks.

When I asked her for three square meals a day, she started to serve waffles every meal.

Garbage

A garbage collector is a man who always has dirty work a' foot.

We have a fine garbage man. He only takes fine garbage. If you have none, he leaves some at your door.

Does she keep a clean house? She's the only one in the neighborhood with wall-to-wall garbage.

Someone stole my garbage bag and, as luck would have it, the police found it and brought it back to me.

We have a fine garbage disposal unit—my uncle. He'll eat anything.

Garden

A garden is a thing of beauty and a job forever.

Last year we ate our whole garden in one meal.

My girl is all thumbs—but at least they're green.

It's autumn and the family that rakes together aches together.

We've solved all our gardening problems. We put in artificial flowers.

They now have a book on gardening called, *Weeder's Digest.*

Did you see the picture of the moon? They must have the same gardener I have.

There's only one thing that will make your lawn look as nice as your neighbors—snow!

Having a green thumb doesn't always mean someone is a good gardener. He could be a lousy painter.

No, I couldn't. You worked so hard all summer in the garden, you eat the pea!

Girls

All the girls like the way I am: single!

By the time I found the girl of my dreams, I was already married.

Most girls with an hourglass figure don't even know the time of day.

There are two kinds of girls: the nice kind and the kind I get.

There are really three kinds of girls: those you look away from, those you look up to, and those you look around.

To most girls, men are not a problem but a solution.

Today a girl has a hard time trying to look as young as her mother.

Bashful? She goes into a closet to change her mind.

Golf

Golf is the most popular method of beating around the bush.

I used to play golf until I lost my ball. The string broke.

I'm thinking of giving up golf. I can't break 90 even when I cheat.

A golfer can walk 10 miles carrying his heavy golf clubs. But at home junior has to bring him the ashtray.

There isn't a good golf course in our town. They all have holes in them.

It's not that I really cheat at golf. I play for my health and a low score makes me feel better.

A fair golfer is one who always quits after 18 holes or 90 strokes, whichever comes first.

Some golfers use carts instead of caddies because carts can't count.

My favorite hole is the 18th. There's nothing like seeing the clubhouse after 18 holes of golf.

Hair

Hair is the only thing that will prevent baldness.

When you intend to blow your top, don't wear a toupee.

I'm not bald. I have flesh-colored hair.

One thing about baldness, it's neat.

I had bad eyesight until I was eight. Then I got a haircut.

She's so tough she uses barbed wire for a hairnet.

She's dyed her hair so many times she has Technicolor dandruff.

He is very sensitive about his hair. I wonder why? He hasn't got any.

He swallowed a firecracker so his hair would grow out in bangs.

You can keep your hair from falling out by knotting it on the inside.

Rubbing hair restorer into your head will give you very hairy fingertips.

Being bald has its advantages: you're the first one to know when it starts raining.

She wanted a simple hair dryer, so I moved her chair closer to the oven.

Nothing keeps a girl's hair so neat as a bashful boyfriend.

She put salt on her wig to make believe she has dandruff.

She had her hair tinted red but now it clashes with her face.

She got an oval hairbrush, but who wants to brush oval hair?

She has black hair and nails to match.

I'm having trouble with my hair. It's waving goodbye!

Lately my hair is getting thin. So what? Who wants fat hair?

But if I *had* a sample of my hair, I wouldn't have to send away for a toupee!

Her hair has changed so often, she has a convertible top.

Hotels

Do you have any suitable accommodations where I can put up with my wife?

The only place I can make a name for myself is in the hotel register.

In Miami they now have a place called "Cadillac Hotel." I think it's only for rich cars.

When people go to summer hotels for a change and rest, the bellboys get the change and the hotel gets the rest.

You can get plenty of hot water in this place. Just ask for soup in the dining room.

If you want to stay overnight, you'll have to make your own bed. Here are the boards and some nails.

They just opened a little hotel near the lake and they call it the Dew Drop Inn.

This hotel is so swanky ...
>   ... it costs you 35 cents to change a quarter.
>   ... even the guests have to use the service entrance.
>   ... you have to wear a tie to go to the swimming pool.
>   ... they butter your toast on both sides.
>   ... they show movies in the elevators.
>   ... they put out a red carpet on the beach.
>   ... you have to wash your hands before using the fingerbowl.

Houses

I come from a broken home. My kids have broken everything in it.

I have a split-level house. I own half and the bank owns the other half.

Everything in our house works with buttons—except my shirts!

I'm not saying our house is old, but we never know when the people upstairs are going to drop in on us.

I'm enlarging my apartment. I'm scraping off the wallpaper.

Mother had to let the maid go, because father wouldn't.

There's no place like home if you haven't got the money to go out.

The only things my wife can fix around the house are Martinis and Manhattans.

There are only two kinds of houses on the market: the kind you don't want and the kind you can't afford.

Dumb? He went looking for lodging with a trombone under one arm and a saxophone under the other.

I don't know who wired our house, but every time the phone rings, the lights dim.

My landlord is always asking me to pay him his rent. To pay *his* rent? I can't even pay my own!

There are two happy days with a new house. The day you buy it and the day you sell it.

We have company in our house every day. The gas company, the mortgage company, and the electric company.

Running water in every room is fine as long as it doesn't come through the roof.

Our house is so old we had to paint it before they could condemn it.

Our house is so big, when it's five o'clock in the living room, it's seven o'clock in the kitchen.

We were offered a house in our price range, but it was in Alaska.

Husband

My husband doesn't know the meaning of fear. But then there are many things he doesn't know.

My husband grew a beard and now he kisses me through a straw.

My husband is absolutely no good at fixing things. So everything in our house works.

A considerate husband is one who remembers to oil the lawnmower for his wife before he goes out to play golf.

Most runaway husbands have been fed too many TV-dinners.

Husbands are like cars. If you take care of them, you don't have to get a new one all the time.

The trouble with a husband who works like a horse is that all he wants to do evenings is hit the hay.

Almost every woman finds a perfect husband. It's usually the man married to her neighbor.

Inflation

Inflation is the time when ...
- ... half your money goes up in smoke, and you need the other half to put out the fire.
- ... you have too much month left over at the end of the money.
- ... you earn $5 an hour and your wife spends $6 a minute at the super-market.
- ... you are able to put $50 worth of groceries into your glove compartment.
- ... you eat three square meals a day and pay for six.
- ... you earn more and more of less and less.
- ... your pockets are full and your stomach isn't.
- ... you can't keep a good price down.
- ... you do more for the dollar than it does for you.
- ... money you haven't got is worth less than before.
- ... prices begin where they used to end.
- ... you look at your nest egg, and it's only chicken feed.

Inflation is a method of cutting a dollar bill in half without damaging the paper.

Inflation is so bad now, I heard a golfer yell "Five!"

Inflation is a shot in the arm that leaves a pain in the neck.

Inflation is something that may be hazardous to your health.

Inflation has turned life into a game of golf: even when you get to the green, you still wind up in the hole.

Inflation has created a brand new economic problem: windfall poverty.

Inflation has changed things. Now one can live as cheaply as two.

Inflation raises everything but hopes.

Inflation being what it is, pretty soon pumpernickel will be a pumperdime.

Inflation has become so bad that it has hit the price of feathers. Even down is up.

Inflation wouldn't be so bad if the prices didn't keep going up.

Inflation wouldn't be so bad if we wouldn't have a depression at the same time.

The real reason so many people are not working is because they are unemployed.

If things get any worse, a pessimist will be anyone who believes an optimist.

The high interest rates are giving many growing concerns growing concern.

Oh, how *are* you? I haven't seen you since hamburger was 39¢ a pound.

The hardest thing to get hold of these days is easy money.

If this isn't a recession, it must be the worst boom in history.

This is the age of enlightenment. Every time I pick up my wallet, it's lighter.

It's no trick to meet expenses. The tough job is to avoid them.

We're living in unusual times. We have pocket calculators, pocket cameras, pocket radios—everything for the pocket but money.

Why didn't they have the depression when everybody was working?

We should try to whip inflation, but who can afford a whip?

Remember the good old days when we had a depression we could afford?

Things are really rough now. I saw a supermarket with a recovery room.

They now have a magazine about inflation; it's called *Payboy*.

Now you can see $10 shoes marked down from $30 to $27.95.

To help inflation and avoid pollution, just buy a new car and then don't drive it.

Fight the rising cost of living: eat at the in-laws!

So eat, drink and be merry for tomorrow it will cost more.

Talking about the high cost of living, the only thing coming down is the rain and even that soaks you.

Kissing

I got a real kick out of kissing her. Her husband caught me.

When some women kiss, they try to make a meal out of it.

She had the kind of lips I like. One on top and one on the bottom.

She had so much bridgework, every time I kissed her I had to pay a toll.

She gives kisses that toast your tonsils.

Anybody can kiss his own wife, but the iceman has his pick.

It takes a lot of experience for a girl to kiss like a beginner.

It's dangerous to awaken your wife with kisses if you're giving them to the maid.

A doctor declared that kissing shortens life. He must have meant single life.

The only time he kisses his wife is when he can't find a napkin.

She asked me if I knew anything about kissing, which was rather odd because I was kissing her at the time.

He is always kissing girls' hands—not that he likes it, but he's crazy about Jergen's lotion.

It's a lot of fun kissing a girl under the mistletoe. It's even more fun kissing her under her nose.

We spent three weeks poking a broom into baby's face to get him used to kissing Grandpa.

It's funny how most girls wait until the kiss is over before they slap the man's face.

Legs

What a figure she has! I've seen better legs on a kitchen table.

How come the girl with the best looking legs always sees the mouse first?

Did I get a shock this morning! I looked at my feet and they were blue—I forgot to take off my socks last night.

Life—Living

I could write the story of my life on a piece of confetti.

Never have so many people lived so well so far behind before.

Into each life some rain must fall—usually on weekends.

Living in the past has one thing in it's favor: it's cheaper.

Life must be worth living. The cost has doubled and we still hang on.

He was fond of high living, so he slept on the roof.

The most wonderful thing made by man: a living for his family.

Anyone who is calm these days probably doesn't feel well.

We should live within our means, even if we have to borrow money to do it.

Twenty years from now you'll be calling these the good times.

Making a living today isn't nearly as hard as living on the living we are making.

Life is so uncertain these days that the only thing you can really count on for sure are your fingers.

Everybody wants to live longer but nobody wants to grow old.

They say people are living longer now. They have to—who can afford to die?

The ladder of life is full of splinters, but you never realize it until you begin to slide down.

Most of us spend a lifetime going to bed when we're not sleepy and getting up when we are.

There's no use worrying about life. It's just a freckle on the nose of time.

What a life! School kids add, rabbits multiply, marriages divide and our days are numbered.

The least understood art is the art of living.

Love

Just give me my golf, the great outdoors and a beautiful girl, and you can keep my golf and the great outdoors.

Sometimes it is better to have loved and lost than to have to do homework for three children.

Do couples matched by computers have to promise not to fold, staple, or punch each other?

Everybody has somebody but all I have is you!

The only cure for love is marriage.

A fork in the road may lead to a spoon in the park.

First she turned my head with her charm and then she turned my stomach with her cooking.

When I take my girl to the movies we always hold hands. She holds hers and I hold mine.

My boyfriend just gave me a ring—it holds 20 keys.

She sends me, and when I get back she's always gone.

The first time I saw her she had moonlight in her hair, starlight in her eyes and a pizza in her mouth.

She was one of the only girls I ever loved, but I can't remember which one.

Well, let me put it this way: if our love affair were on TV, I'd switch channels.

I had to propose to her in the garage. I couldn't back out.

Just because a fellow says he'll call you up is no sign that he'll give you a ring.

Man

By the time a man fully understands women, he's not interested anymore.

For every man there is a woman, and he's lucky if his wife never finds out.

Take it like a man. Blame everything on your wife.

This is still a free country where every man can do as his wife pleases.

All men are created free and equal; then they grow up and get married.

A family man is a man who has replaced the money in his wallet with pictures of his wife and kids.

There are three kinds of men who will never understand women: young men, middle-aged men, and old men.

Every man expects his wife to be a sweetheart, a cook, a laundress, a valet, an attentive audience, a seamstress, and a nurse.

Men generally fall into three categories: the handsome, the clever, and the majority.

Marriage

There's a lot to be said about marriage, but who has the nerve?

I'm the result of mixed marriage. My father was a man and my mother was a woman.

Research told us that 50% of all married people are wives.

Am I happily married? I'll bet you don't have a wife who worships and adores you. Well, neither have I.

I like to run my home like a ship with me as the captain. Too bad I married an admiral.

After going steady for 12 years, we broke our engagement and got married.

The early part of our marriage was wonderful. The trouble started when we were leaving the church.

Am I happily married? Every morning when I leave for work I always shake hands with my wife.

It was a May and December romance. She wanted to get married in May and he wanted to call it off in December.

She's so busy planning her fourth wedding, she doesn't have time to cook for her third husband.

My best friend married my sister; now he hates me like a brother.

I remember when and where I got married, but what escapes me is why?

Marriages are made in heaven. But so is thunder and lightning.

Money

The only thing you can get without money is sick.

You can't have a race without race horses, but you sure can have money trouble without money.

Rich? He has bills with pictures of presidents you probably never heard of.

Looks can be deceiving. A dollar bill looks the same as it did 10 years ago.

The real trouble with money is that you can't use it more than once.

Whether you are rich or poor, it's nice to have money.

Money isn't everything, but it's sure a cure for poverty.

The dollar has now shrunk to the point where we should call it a dollarette.

Money can't buy happiness, but have you tried to buy anything without it?

Our floating currency is a sign of sinking economy.

Anybody who can afford to pay the interest rates these days doesn't need a bank loan.

You never know the real value of money until you try to borrow some.

It doesn't matter if you are born poor and die poor as long as you're rich in between.

There is plenty of money around these days. The trouble is, everyone owes it to someone else.

The other day I tried to get change for a quarter and it cost me 34 cents.

There are bigger things in life than money: bills.

The reason coins are round is because they were made to circulate.

Some day I hope to be able to afford to spend as much as I do now.

I don't know where my money is coming from, but my wife sure knows where it's going.

His credit rating is so bad, his *money* isn't even accepted.

Money isn't important as long as you have it.

Movies

The movie was so bad it curdled the butter on my popcorn.

I went to a drive-in movie and somebody stole my car.

The movie was so crowded even the ushers were standing.

The picture was so bad, people were standing in line to get out.

I never go to a picture unless I've seen it before. Then I know it's good.

Some movies would be better if they shot less film and more actors.

I was so disgusted with the picture I walked out the third time I saw it.

I took my wife to see a movie. It was the longest time we've spent together since our honeymoon.

Some of today's pictures are so long, it takes less time to read the book.

This movie had a surprise ending. Just when you think it will never end, it does.

He now has a leading part in the theater—he's a head usher.

The happiest ending in the movies is when the person behind you finishes his popcorn.

Because of the unusually suspenseful nature of this film, no one will be permitted in the theater.

Wouldn't it be nice if you could go to the movies and see a picture as good as the one that's coming next week?

Music

He is very musical. As a child he played on the floor, now he plays on the piano.

I have music in my veins. I just wish I had blood.

He is such a bad musician, when he plays the National Anthem people sit down.

We played Brahms here yesterday. Brahms lost.

He can play the Minute Waltz in forty seconds.

Some piano players should be moving them instead.

They laughed when I sat down at the piano. Someone had removed the bench.

He had a three-piece combo: an organ, a cup and a monkey.

He composes music in bed. He calls it sheet music.

How come you look so sharp and play so flat?

They laughed when I picked up the violin. They didn't know I was from the finance company.

I know he is a musician, but what does he do for a living?

He plays the violin exactly like Heifetz. Under his chin.

To play the harp like an angel you've got to practice like the devil.

This band consists of six pieces: one piano player and five sheets of music.

Today he is going to play like he never played before—in tune!

He is a considerate pianist. He always wears gloves when he plays so as not to disturb his neighbors.

He has a great ear for music. Too bad he hasn't got the voice for it.

He was studying music for three years. Now he can read music but not play it.

They formed this band about three years ago. It's about time they started to play together.

Names

If you have twins and they're girls, call them Kate and Duplicate.

I never remember a name but I always forget a face.

They now have a magazine for farmers, called *Breeder's Digest*.

He is so polite, he always takes his hat off whenever someone mentions his name.

He even changed his name to Hilton so it would match the name on the towels.

My grandfather is great. I call him my great grandfather.

I call my wife "Daily"; otherwise she would get suspicious.

I'm sure we met; I can't remember your face but I never forget a dress.

My brother changed his name to "Exit" because he likes to see his name in lights.

A man who crosses the ocean twice without taking a bath is called a dirty double-crosser.

She calls it a purse, but I call it a portable attic.

He bought some shirts cheap and changed his name to fit the monogram.

It got so bad I didn't have a dime to my name, so I changed my name.

I don't worry about talking in my sleep. My wife and my girlfriend have the same name.

When a girl calls you by your first name, she's out for your last.

You can call a woman a kitten but not a cat, a mouse but not a rat, a chicken but not a hen, a duck but not a goose, a vision but not a sight.

Party

Their parties are so formal and stiff. She is so formal and he gets so stiff.

Social tact is making your company feel at home, even though you wish they were.

We went to a baseball party. That's one where all the bases are loaded.

A dull party has one advantage: you can go to bed at a decent hour.

What? You think this party is noisy? Just wait till our guests arrive.

My uncle wants to start a third party. He was thrown out of two last night.

People

There are two kinds of people: those who like to get up in the morning and the rest of us.

There are really three kinds of people: those who make things happen, those who watch things happen, and those who don't know what's happening.

People used to settle their problems over coffee and cigarettes. Now that's their problem.

Half the people in Washington are hoping to be discovered, and the other half are afraid they will be.

Photography

After he looked at his passport photo he decided he looked so bad, he better stay home and rest.

He works in a factory testing cameras. They take his picture to see how much the camera can take.

Of course you don't look natural in this photo. The photographer asked you to look pleasant.

This photographer was so poor he couldn't afford a darkroom, so he wore a blindfold.

It takes about two days at sea to make travelers look like their passport photos.

Police

Say, officer, can a man be arrested for striking a match?

He is now a police reporter. Twice a week he has to report to the police.

The only time you can spit in a policeman's face is when his beard is on fire.

This burglar has become so successful, he stopped making house calls.

Dad is always bothered by flat feet. They keep giving him parking tickets.

Officer, where do I go to apologize for shooting my husband?

I call the policeman "Drummer" because he is always on the beat.

In our house crime went from the sixth floor down to the third floor.

Sorry Madame, I can't arrest a man for loitering in his own home.

Pollution

The air was so bad this summer, I had to buy three air conditioners: two died of air poisoning.

The fog was so thick, we couldn't see the pollution.

The smog was so thick, I took a deep breath and chipped a tooth.

The smog was so bad, even the Smith Brothers were coughing.

The smog was so dense, the plane landed on a gray cloud thinking it was the air field.

If the fog ever lifts, we'll be able to see the smog.

It was so foggy, he milked his cow fourteen minutes until he found out he was squeezing his own fingers.

His new house has big windows all around; now he gets wall-to-wall pollution.

New York air is nothing to sniff at!

People in Los Angeles have a wonderful diet. They eat only when the air is clear.

It was so bad, they had to put windshield wipers on bicycles.

People now talk through their noses—they're afraid to open their mouths.

I remember when "Smoke Gets In Your Eyes" was a song and not a weather report.

Last night I took a deep breath and then asked for a toothpick.

Our sky is much clearer than in London because we have more skyscrapers.

On a clear day I can see the stores across the street.

I shot an arrow into the air and it got stuck there.

Spring must be here. The smog is turning green.

Pollution is getting worse. I put air in my tires and they coughed.

There was so much pollution, my tires were wearing out from the inside.

Pollution has become so bad, we now pray: Give Us This Day Our Daily Breath!

Pollution? Three firemen were treated for smoke poisoning and they were answering a false alarm.

The pollution was so dense, they put up the street signs in Braille.

Air pollution doesn't bother my wife. She doesn't stop talking long enough to take a deep breath.

If pollution gets any worse, we'll be saying, "One Nation, Invisible...."

The air pollution was so thick a kid built a smog man.

I want air pollution; I don't trust clean air. I like to see what I'm breathing in.

Water pollution was started by dumping all that tea into the ocean in Boston.

If the pollution keeps increasing, there won't be enough smog to go around.

To survive pollution, you have to breathe West and cough East.

Our government wants to do something about pollution—as soon as they can see their way clear.

The only good thing about polluted air is that it's better than no air at all.

The air isn't too bad if you chew on it for a while before you swallow.

The air is so thick now, you can feel it.

The air is getting so polluted these days that people are coughing outside of churches, too.

The air was so bad, the statue in Central Park was coughing.

Popularity

Popular? They gave him a Testimonial Dinner and nobody showed up.

Socially she is the creme de la crumb.

Popular? People forget him while they're shaking his hand.

Post Office

He is a man of letters. He works for the post office.

Our mailman is so lazy he stopped making house calls.

Instead of raising the price of the postage stamps, why don't they just use smaller stamps?

Postage is so high now, every time you mail a get-well card you get sick.

Poverty

We didn't live on the wrong side of the tracks. We lived *on* the tracks.

Cheer up. The less you have the more there is to get.

My Dad couldn't afford a bicycle for me, so he took off the *B* and gave me an icicle.

For my birthday I used to get a picture of a birthday cake.

My mother bought one meatball and made hamburger for all of us.

Burglars used to break into our house and leave things.

When we once got a loaf of bread, we had to ask how to cut it.

Restaurant

The food here is so bad, they always serve Pepto-Bismol for dessert.

Every time they have a wedding here, they serve rice pudding the next day.

They serve a dish so foreign you have to eat it with an interpreter.

The sign said, "Watch your hat and coat." And while I was doing that, someone stole my steak.

They serve cakes here just like mother used to make, just before they took Dad to the hospital.

In many places the food is frozen and the waitress is fresh.

Say, waiter, put the rest of this steak in a doggie bag and add some bread in case he wants a sandwich.

I asked the waiter what I could get for a dollar and he gave me four quarters.

The food here was so bad, the other side of the menu was a prescription blank.

This restaurant honors all cards—even Blue Cross.

I like a dim restaurant. By the time the waiter finds the 25¢ tip, you're gone.

I went to a weight-watcher's place and while I was watching my weight, someone stole my coat.

This place is so expensive, for an after-dinner mint you need the one in Denver.

Secretary

I call her "Switchboard" because when she walks all her lines are busy.

Sure, I can write shorthand, but it takes a little longer!

When a man is always late for dinner, either his wife is a poor cook, or his secretary is very pretty.

I just heard that lipstick is poison. From now on I'll kiss my secretary through a straw.

My secretary asked me for a new pen. The old one is beginning to make mistakes.

My secretary can do 30 words a minute. No, not typing—reading.

My secretary has a perfect attendance record—she hasn't missed a coffee break in three years.

My secretary can take shorthand, type 60 words a minute and take your mind off the stock market.

My secretary never makes the same mistake twice. She always comes up with new ones.

My secretary warned me, if I don't give her a raise she'll start wearing long skirts.

My boss just hired another secretary. Now he has one for each knee.

"Our automatic answering service is out of order. This is the secretary speaking!"

"Say, boss, I need a new typewriter; this one makes too many mistakes."

A confidential secretary is one your wife never finds out about.

We already have noiseless typewriters. Now if we only could get noiseless secretaries.

"I have been wanting to meet you; my husband told me so little about you!"

Every time I come up with a fresh idea, my secretary slaps me.

My wife doesn't care what my secretary looks like, just as long as he's efficient.

A good secretary is one who can keep up with her boss when he's dictating and ahead of him when he's not.

Some secretaries are very punctual. They come in exactly a half an hour late every day.

He had a peach of a secretary until his wife canned her.

When a secretary marries the boss, she gives up being a secretary and he gives up being the boss.

"My dear girl, I don't know how you do it. You've been with us only a week and you're already a month behind in your work!"

Sickness

Doctor, I'm sick and tired of being sick and tired!

What does one send a sick florist?

No wonder he has a cold. He has a hole in his head.

He has a bad allergy. He is allergic to work.

The only thing he can keep in his head is a cold.

I've been nursing a grouch all night. My wife is sick.

Sickness comes in four stages: Ill, Pill, Bill and Will.

Nobody is sicker than the man who is sick on his day off.

I sure hope I'm sick. I'd hate to feel like this when I'm well.

She sneezed in her tomato soup and we thought she had the measles.

We don't get ulcers from what we eat but from what's eating us.

Although he was never fatally ill before, he woke up dead.

Pneumonia isn't bad as long you don't let it develop into a cold.

I was finally cured of that pain in my back. I found out my suspenders were twisted.

I ate in some place yesterday and actually got something free: instant indigestion.

He even gets seasick on the Staten Island Ferry and airsick on a merry-go-round.

Singing

Her voice is too loud for indoor use.

This girl can be had for a song: the Wedding March.

Sing? Her voice is flatter than her nose.

She couldn't carry a tune if it had a handle.

The best thing about a popular song is it's not popular very long.

She went on stage to sing "Goodbye My Love" and they all went.

Sure, I like opera, but not all the singing.

He is an old folk singer. He sings only to old folks.

Just wait till you hear her sing. You won't be able to take your eyes off her voice.

The last time she sang, all the dogs in the neighborhood came to our house.

They laughed when I stood up to sing. How did I know I was under the table?

Just because she has legs like a canary doesn't mean she can sing!

You'll have to excuse her. Her voice is changing from bad to terrible.

She sings with heart and soul. She should try it with her voice sometime.

Can she sing? I've heard better music come out of a leaky balloon.

At a party, why is it always the person who can't sing who does?

Now if you think this song is old, wait until you see the girl who sings it.

I once wrote some songs that were so bad, I had to rewrite them before I could throw them away.

A quartet is a group of four, each of whom thinks the other three can't sing.

She's got a very fine voice. It ought to be fine. Every time she sings, she strains it.

She really has an unusual voice. It's like asthma set to music.

Sleeping

I missed my nap today. I slept right through it.

Every morning I wake up with a nagging headache: my wife.

I'm allergic to sleeping pills. They make me drowsy.

I know I snore, but only when I sleep.

Ma, don't send my brother to wake me up when he has a hammer in his hand!

Smile and the world smiles with you. Snore, and you snore alone!

Insomnia wouldn't be so bad if I wouldn't lie awake worrying about it.

Why do people who snore always fall asleep first?

He is such an insomniac that when he's asleep, he dreams he's not sleeping.

Last night I found two feet of ice in my bed—both belonged to my wife.

Sleep never seems so important at night as it does in the morning.

Many people spend money on pills to sleep and coffee to stay awake.

Stock Market

Even my blue chips are turning green.

Some stocks split, mine just crumble.

I invested my money in the market now: fruits and vegetables!

I have an unusual stock broker. He specializes in stock losses.

I know a conceited stock broker who has a blue chip on his shoulder.

I own a great deal of Penny Stock. Too bad I bought it for three dollars.

If you want to see the Stock Market hit a new high, hold the chart upside down.

This week I'm doing fine on the market. My broker is on vacation.

Supermarket

Nothing goes faster than a $10 bill in a supermarket.

When my wife goes to the supermarket, she has shelf-control.

I took my paycheck to the supermarket and watched it self-destruct.

A young bride tried to squeeze a can of tomatoes to see if it was fresh.

A supermarket is a place where you can find anything but your children.

The high cost of living doesn't bother me when I enter the supermarket. It's the high cost of leaving!

Talking

She talks so much her tongue gets tired.

My wife can say more in a look than I can in a book.

I have never seen her tongue. It moves so fast.

She talks like a revolving door.

When I talk, my wife listens—to the radio, to the record player, to the TV set.

The only time my wife stops talking is when her mother starts.

I wouldn't say my wife talks a lot, but I had laryngitis for two weeks and she never noticed.

It's not what a man says that counts, it's what a woman answers.

Her mouth never gets 8 hours' sleep.

She has an impediment in her speech. It's always two hours too long.

Waiting for a woman to finish talking is like waiting for the end of a roller towel.

I don't mind that my wife always has the last word. It's the waiting for it that I hate.

She talks so much that every month she has to go and have her tonsils retreaded.

We had a power failure in our house. My wife lost her voice.

I will never repeat gossip, so please listen carefully the first time.

Anybody who had to listen to my wife talking has had occasion to use aspirin.

Of course, there is a lot to be said in her favor, but it's not nearly as interesting.

It isn't so much what a woman says that hurts. It's the number of times she says it.

The first thing she will do in the morning is brush her teeth and sharpen her tongue.

Taxes

A tax collector is a man looking for untold wealth.

Well, income tax day has come and gone. And so has my money.

After paying my taxes all I have left is a deficit.

Taxes are what you have to pay for doing okay.

It is hard to believe that America was founded to avoid taxes.

When it comes to paying income taxes, some people think filing means chiseling.

Things could be worse. What if the Tax Office started charging for the tax forms?

I have no trouble filing my income tax. But I have trouble paying it.

I'm putting all my money in taxes—the only thing sure to go up.

The tax collector must like poor people. Because he's creating so many of them.

Now they have a tax on funerals. I'd die before I'd pay that!

Did you notice that the tax forms are shorter this year? And so is my income.

No matter how bad a child is, he's still good for a tax exemption.

Did you notice that as the world gets smaller, it takes more taxes to keep it together?

We used to have no tax after income, but now we have no income after taxes.

Everything I have I owe—to the Internal Revenue.

The way he squawks about paying taxes, you'd think he does.

I just paid all my taxes and I'm worried. I still have some money left.

He discovered a wonderful way to avoid taxes. He doesn't work.

I pay income tax like a strip-teaser. I take off as much as the law allows.

When a man doesn't gripe about taxes, he's either very rich or very poor.

Taxi

This cab driver gave up his job because so many people talked behind his back.

Traffic jam? I once sat in a cab for 20 minutes and the only thing moving was the meter.

Taxies are doing fine now. On every corner they now have a blinking sign: Don't Walk!

Teacher

My teacher has a reading problem. He can't read my writing.

My teacher really loves me. He kept me in his class for three years.

My history teacher is so old, she doesn't teach history; she remembers it.

Teeth

He can't help being stupid. He got cavities in his wisdom teeth.

They now have a toothpaste with food particles for people who get hungry while brushing.

Now I know why she smiles all the time. Her teeth are the only things that aren't wrinkled.

Telephone

It is no fun to kiss a girl over the phone unless you are right in the booth with her.

My Dad was very strict. We weren't allowed to answer the phone until it rang.

Telephoning is just like marriage. You don't always get the right party.

I'm very famous. My name is even mentioned in one of the biggest books ever published: the telephone book.

My wife's laryngitis has cost the phone company a fortune.

My wife tries hard to keep a clean house, but yesterday the phone rang and she couldn't find it.

Television

I'm in favor of longer commercials on TV. It's the only chance I get to read my evening paper.

My Dad wants to go on television. It's the only way he can get into 200 bars at the same time.

Nowadays you have to be a success on radio before you can become a failure on television.

Say, shall we watch the 6 o'clock news and get indigestion or wait for the 11 o'clock news and get insomnia?

Today a minuteman is a man who can dash into the kitchen, prepare a sandwich and be back before the TV commercial is over.

A TV sponsor is a man who watches the commercials and goes to the kitchen for food during the show.

She'd leave her husband but he's always watching TV and he wouldn't notice it.

On those TV medical shows you can see them cut out appendix and tonsils, but never the commercials.

I never thought TV could cause anti-social behavior. Then my repairman handed me his bill.

Television gives me nothing to do when I'm not doing anything.

Television has made a semicircle out of the family circle.

Television is a wonderful thing. You meet so many people—mostly repairmen.

Television is a wonderful medium. Imagine being able to reach millions of people who can't reach you.

Television is a wonderful invention. It lets you watch a ten-year-old movie for only $300.

Television permits you to be entertained in your living room by characters you wouldn't ordinarily allow in your living room.

A TV set is an instrument with a picture in front, a loudspeaker on the side and an installment behind.

Did you notice that families on TV shows never watch television?

We never go out. I sit at the TV set and smoke and my wife sits beside me and fumes.

I have trouble with my new color TV every month. I can't make the payments.

How come on TV the people always find parking space in front of a bank?

All right, all right! I'll make you supper during the next commercial.

I've been seeing 3-D pictures on TV for a long time: dull, dark and dated.

I'm now putting a kid through college. It's the son of my TV repairman.

There are so few books in our house that if the TV breaks down, we'll have to talk to each other.

Movies on TV are like furniture. They're either early American or Old English.

This repairman is so fast, he fixed my set before he could say $60.

I find TV very educating. Everytime my wife turns on the set, I go into the next room and read a book.

The only thing we can definitely get on our TV set is dust.

This TV station is so small, it can only be watched in their studio.

Texas

A Texan is a man who makes money from oil and spends it like water.

The best description of Texas: miles, miles and miles.

In Texas the station wagons are bigger than the stations.

Remember when Texas was a state and not a parking lot for Cadillacs?

One Texan is so rich, he has wall-to-wall carpeting on his range.

One Texas child likes to play with blocks, so his father bought him Rockefeller Center.

Texas newsboys are so rich, their chauffeurs deliver the papers.

One Texan learned how to fly his little airplane in his living room.

A Texas cowboy doesn't brand his cattle, he engraves them.

One Texan had a terrible nightmare. Dreamt he had only one million.

There was that Cadillac dealer in Texas who gave away Volkswagens as free samples.

He bought his son a cowboy outfit: 50,000 acres, 5000 head of cattle, and 1000 horses.

When one Texan was prospecting for oil, all the others sent him get-well cards.

Thanksgiving

I always call the turkey "Napoleon," since I always get the boney part.

The trouble with Thanksgiving dinners is that after you eat one, you get hungry again two days later.

Our last turkey was so tough, every time we shut the oven, he blew out the pilot light.

At Thanksgiving what does a turkey have to be thankful for?

We were so poor, at Thanksgiving we looked at a picture of a turkey.

Travel

Traveling brings something in your life you never had before: poverty!

Nothing makes traveling so broadening as the meals.

New York is a fine place to visit if you're flying over it in a plane.

A typical tourist is one who doesn't want to be considered a typical tourist.

Tourists spend most of their time taking pictures so they can get home and finally see what they saw.

Tourists are people who climb a 7000-foot mountain to put a dime in a telescope so they can see where they came from.

Trouble

He has so many troubles that if anything bad happens, he has to postpone it a few weeks.

Trouble? My wife left me two weeks ago but my mother-in-law didn't.

I'm in real trouble now. My boss told me to put more life into my stories and I write the obituaries.

You think you have troubles? What about the deep sea diver coming up, who passed his ship going down?

Vacation

Are you looking forward to your vacation, or are you taking your wife along?

Summer vacation usually puts the kids in the pink and Daddy in the red.

On my last vacation it was raining day and night—until I found out I was sleeping in a carwash.

He went through the fog of London, motored through Spain, cycled through France, waltzed through Vienna and skidded through Greece.

Vacation usually consists of 2 weeks, which are 2 short, after which you are 2 tired to return 2 work and 2 broke not 2.

When my wife is away on vacation, the whole house is empty but the sink is full of dishes.

Just spend your vacation in your backyard and your friends will know what you are: sensitive, home-loving and broke.

Europe is wonderful. If you ever go there, don't miss it.

Wedding

I never like June weddings. They can ruin a summer vacation.

For a bride a wedding means showers. For the groom it means curtains.

Nobody ever gives a groom a shower because he'll be in hot water soon enough.

Weddings have become so expensive, that now it's the father who breaks down and cries.

If you invite only married couples to your wedding, the presents are clear profit.

"Are you a friend of the bride, the groom or the caterer?"

Women

Most women are either trying to put on weight, take it off, or rearrange it.

When a woman suffers in silence, it means her phone is out of order.

Every woman looks beautiful after a few drinks.

I don't play around with women. When it comes to women I'm not playing.

Many women today are not as young as they are painted.

Two percent of all women are misinformed. The rest have phones.

The only thing most women regret about their past is the length.

The average woman can talk faster than any husband can listen.

No woman is ever so hoarse that she can't talk about it.

Nothing ages a woman more than having her friends guess how old she is.

When a woman begins to show her age, she begins to hide it.

Generally speaking, women are mostly generally speaking.

There is only one bad woman in the world and every husband thinks she is his wife.

Now that I finally understand women, my wife won't let me out of the house.

Woman Driver

When a woman driver puts her hand out the window, it's a sure sign she is going to do something.

"Don't worry dear. It's only a scratched fender. You can look at it in the trunk!"

When she parks the car she always plays the radio very loud so she won't hear the crash.

"Don't tell me the carburetor is dirty. I had the car washed yesterday!"

She wouldn't go near her car when she heard the gears were stripped. She was too modest.

They now have cars built especially for women. The fenders are inside.

Oh boy, can my wife drive. You should see her tickets!

"Look honey, the fender's been acting up again!"

She is a very careful and slow driver. Only once did she get a parking ticket on the George Washington Bridge.

My wife is a careful driver. She always drives on the sidewalk just to avoid traffic.

I respect women drivers. I always give them half of the road just as soon as I figure out which half they want.

Work

No wife of *mine* is going to work. I'm afraid to stay home alone.

The only thing you can get without working is hungry.

It takes some people an hour to get to work—after they get there.

She used to work for her husband until she got him.

My new job is killing me. It's hard work, day after day. But I'm glad it's permanent.

The reason worry kills more people than work is that more people worry than work.

It is wise to learn a trade; then you will always know what kind of work you are out of.

These days if you want to relax you really have to work for it.

Writing

There is a book for people who disagree: a contradictionary.

I just bought a new pen: it writes under water.

So many people wanted my autograph, I had to learn how to write.

Can he write? He has something Shakespeare never had—a typewriter!

A banker may write a bad poem and get away with it. But just let a poet write a bad check.

It is silly to spend six months writing a novel when you can buy one for three dollars.

The only thing he can do better than anybody else is to read his own writing.

2

———

Crazy Jokes

Zany Jokes

One-Liners

Jokes like that will make humor illegal.

A sense of humor is the ability to laugh at your own jokes when your wife tells them.

This is a Polaroid joke. It takes one minute to get the whole picture.

Did you hear Whistler's Mother is missing? She's off her rocker.

In Africa you can see a man-eating lion, and in a delicatessen you can see a man eating herring.

Conductor! Conductor! Let me off this train, I thought it was a lunch wagon.

George! You blow on your soup. You don't fan it with your hat!

See, I told you tomatoes don't bounce.

Two-Liners

A pig was never known to wash.
No, but I have seen a pig iron.

Are you a coffee perker?
No, I'm a teabag dipper.

Are you a cross-town bus?
No, I'm a bus driver.

Are you a good comedian?
I don't know. Every time I talk people laugh at me.

Are you an avid reader?
No, I never read avid.

Are you very musical?
Sure, I have drums in my ears.

Aren't you going to straighten out the room?
Why, is it crooked?

But Dad, I don't want to go to Europe.
Shut up and keep rowing.

Can a man be in two places at the same time?
Certainly. Last week I was staying in Nebraska and I was homesick all the time.

Can February March?
No, but April May.

Can I have a meal on the cuff?
Yes, let's start with some soup on your lap.

Can you sing high C?
No, I sing low-sy!

Can you sing "Night and Day"?
No, I tire easily.

Could you pass the salt?
I think I can. I move pianos for a living.

Daddy, I have only two cavities.
Here, have a dollar and get two more.

Did the nurse take your temperature?
So far only my wallet is missing.

Did you ever swim in the nude?
No, only in water.

Did you ever stand on a pet?
Sure, on a carpet.

Did you ever touch a live wire?
No, but I heard it's a shocking experience.

Did you mail out those circulars?
No, I couldn't find any round envelopes.

Do you file your nails?
No, I cut them off and throw them away.

Do you have a riding habit?
I do; my habit is to ride on top of a horse.

Do you have any trouble with your nose?
Yes, doctor, it's always in the way when I take off my T-shirt.

Do you like Kipling?
I don't know. I never kippled.

Do you like meatballs?
I don't think I ever attended any.

Do you remember when you were born?
No, I was too young.

Do you serve crabs here?
Sure, sit right down.

Doc, do you think oysters are healthy?
Well, I never heard any complain.

Doc, what's good for biting fingernails?
Sharp teeth.

Doctor, I just swallowed my harmonica.
Calm down, be glad you didn't play the piano.

Doctor, I'm in agony.
No you're in my office.

Doctor, my liver is no good.
How is your bacon?

Does beer make you smart?
I don't know, but it made Budweiser.

Does water always come through the ceiling like that?
No, only when it rains.

Does your watch tell time?
No, you have to look at it.

Eat your spinach, it will put color in your cheeks.
But who wants green cheeks?

Eating, hey!
No, it's spaghetti!

Has your tooth stopped aching?
I don't know. My dentist kept it.

Have you any blue neckties to match my eyes?
No, but we have some soft hats to match your head.

Have you had your iron today?
Well, I've bitten my nails.

Haven't I seen you somewhere before?
Yes, I have been somewhere before.

He has his two feet planted firmly on the ground.
That's very nice, but how does he get his pants off?

Hello, plumber, I have a drip in the kitchen.
Don't blame me. You married him!

His mustache made me laugh.
Yes, it tickled me too.

Honey, there's a peddler here with a mustache.
Tell him we don't need any.

How come your dog has a flat nose?
He's always chasing parked cars.

How could you hit yourself on the forehead?
I stood on a chair.

How did you find America?
I turned left at Greenland.

How did you like the bath salts, madame?
There're very good tasting, but a real bath is so much better.

How did you like your trip to the zoo with Daddy?
It was real great. One animal paid $20 across the board.

How did you sleep last night?
Oh, lying down, as usual.

How did your girl like your new mustache?
Oh, I forget to show it to her.

How do you feel about Flushing, New York?
I think it's a great idea.

How do you prevent infection caused by biting insects?
Don't bite any.

How do you want your medicine today?
With a fork.

How many members does your club have?
All of them.

I can lie in bed in the morning and watch the sun rise.
That's nothing. I can sit in the living room and see the kitchen sink.

I can turn a paper into a flower.
That's nothing. I can go to the corner and turn into a drugstore.

I can't float a loan.
I can't swim either.

I get paid by the hour.
I get paid by the bank.

I had the radio on all night.
Really? How did it fit?

I have a big corn on the bottom of my foot.
That's a fine place for it. Nobody can step on it but you.

I have a case of laryngitis.
Open it up. I drink anything.

I just bought a waffle iron. Now we can have waffles.
I don't think I ever ate ironed waffles.

I kept regular hours for ten years.
What were you in for?

I'd like to buy some DDT, please.
How do you spell it?

I love you terribly.
Everything you do you do terribly.

I once had to live on a can of beans for a whole week.
My goodness! Weren't you afraid of falling off?

I once swallowed a watch.
Wasn't that time-consuming?

I play piano by ear.
Doesn't it interfere with your earrings?

I saw some bad news on the TV lately.
It must be your antenna.

I saw your wife at the dog show.
And how did she compare to the other dogs?

I see you are sweeping out the room.
No, I am sweeping out the dirt, and leaving the room.

I think you have acute appendicitis.
Thank you, doctor. Now how about the sharp pain in my stomach?

I throw myself into everything I undertake.
Go dig a deep well.

I want a pair of alligator shoes.
What size does your alligator wear?

I was a life saver last summer.
Really? What flavor?

I wish they'd turn up the light. I can't hear so well in the dark.
I know what you mean. I can't hear so well over the phone without my glasses.

I wouldn't worry. You're sound as a dollar.
Wow, Doc, you sure know how to hurt a guy.

I'm a big collector. Now I collect flies.
Yes, I read about you in the fly paper.

I'm going on a safari to Africa.
Drop us a lion now and then.

I'm looking for a small boy with one eye.
Well, if he's very small you'd better use both eyes.

I'm looking for an apartment.
Which way did it go?

I'm 6 feet 4 with my hat on.
I'm 7 feet 9 with my umbrella up.

I'm so sore from running that I can't stand or sit.
If you're telling the truth, you're lying.

If I had 3 apples and ate one, how many would I have left?
Three. One inside and two outside.

I've been trying to think of a word for two weeks.
How about fortnight?

Is my wife home?
No, who shall I say called?

Is your dog housebroken?
Sure. He broke three houses last week.

It took me 30 minutes to write a note to the milk man.
Next time write on the paper before you put it in the bottle.

John, the bill collector is here.
Okay, give him the stack on my desk.

Last night I had a date for dinner.
So? Usually you have a prune.

Look! That mountain over there is 4,000 feet high.
Gee, from here it looks like it touches the ground.

May I have some ice water?
Peel an onion; that will make your eyes water.

May I haunt your castle?
Be my ghost.

My father died from drinking shellac.
Well, one thing, he had a nice finish.

My father is a doctor; I can be sick for nothing.
My father is a preacher; I can be good for nothing.

My father has a Washington shoe.
That's nothing. My father has an Adam's apple.

Mommy, there's a man at the door with a package marked C.O.D.
Sounds fishy to me!

My wife can play the saxophone, paint and write music.
What other defects does she have?

My wife drives me to drink.
You are lucky. Mine makes me walk.

My wife has a big stomach but she said she's gonna diet.
What color?

My uncle has a wooden leg.
My aunt has a cedar chest.

Oh, I see, you have water on your knees.
Yes, doctor. I just spilled a whole glass.

On which side of the cup should the handle be?
On the outside.

Pardon me, what time is it?
Tell *me*, and we'll both know.

Please don't spit on the floor.
Why not? Does it leak?

Say, conductor, can I take this train to New Jersey?
No, it's much too heavy.

Say, dad, where are the Alps?
Ask mother, she puts everything away.

Say, did you catch all those fish yourself?
No, I had a little worm helping me.

Say, is my face clean enough to eat?
Yes, but you better use your hands.

Say, son, what does this C mean on your report card?
Colossal!

Say, where did you get that red lantern?
I just found it in the big hole in the ground.

Should I stir the coffee with my left hand?
No, use a spoon.

So your birthday is June 10th. What year?
Every year!

Stop making faces at the bulldog.
He started it!

Stop poking the baby.
I'm not poking. I'm only counting his measles.

That's a nice house you bought. But where is the door?
Are you planning to go somewhere?

Tell me, does your friend have a mustache?
I don't think so. If he does, he keeps it shaved off.

Tell me, what's up there, the sun or the moon?
Don't ask me, I'm a stranger myself.

There's a man outside with a wooden leg named Smith.
What's the name of the other leg?

They say Bill always keeps his word.
He has to. No one else will take it.

This brandy is a hundred years old.
It is? It tastes like new.

This coffee is imported from Brazil.
You don't say! And it's still warm.

This parrot is sixty years old.
He's awful green for his age.

Waiter, the menu says cold boiled ham. What is cold boiled ham?
Ham boiled in cold water.

Waiter, this boiled egg is hard as a rock.
I don't know why, sir. It's been cooking all morning.

Waiter, this pudding tastes like plaster.
Yes, sir, that's why we charge ceiling prices.

We just bought a Rembrandt.
How many cylinders?

What are those frozen band-aids for?
Cold cuts.

What are you knitting?
A cover for my hot-water bottle.

What are you taking for your cold?
I don't know. How much will you give me?

What do they call a hospital for parrots?
Polly clinic.

What do they call a mother who eats crackers in bed?
A crummy mummy.

What do they do with doughnut holes?
They use them to stuff macaroni.

What do you think of Czechoslovakia?
Well, it's hard to say.

What does a 500-pound parrot say?
Polly wants a cracker, NOW!

What have you got on the radio?
Oh, just a little dust.

What have you in the shape of bananas today?
Cucumbers, lady!

What happened to the man who killed the goose that laid the golden egg?
I guess his goose was cooked.

What happened to the Morris chair?
Morris took it back.

What is the name of your bank?
Piggy.

What ruined your marriage?
The wedding.

What? This diamond ring costs only $2.50. How can you afford to sell it so cheap?
I took out the stone.

What would you call a smart duck?
A wise quacker.

What would you do if I criticized your figure?
I would hold it against you.

What would you like to be when you grow up?
Oh, about 6 foot 3.

What's the idea of kicking my bucket of water over?
I just wanted to see how it feels to kick the bucket.

What's the weather like outside?
I can't see. It's too cloudy.

What's your hobby, Doctor?
Oh, I'm getting lots of pleasure mailing out my bills.

When you were in London did you see them changing the guards?
Why? Were they dirty?

Where was Solomon's temple?
On the side of his head.

Why are you cleaning up the spilled coffee with cake?
It's sponge cake, isn't it?

Why are you conducting the band looking at the audience?
I'm afraid to face the music.

Why are you crying?
My teeth stepped on my tongue.

Why are you hitting that old lady?
I'm trying to help her across the street and she doesn't want to go.

Why are you pulling the rope?
Did you ever try to push one?

Why are you putting that calendar in your piggy bank?
I want to save time.

Why are you so excited?
I cut this board three times and it's still too short.

Why are you standing in a puddle of water?
I'm trying to stamp out a hotfoot.

Why are you wearing a fireman's hat and a bathing suit?
I promised my girl I'd go through fire and water for her.

Why did you get fired from the Tea Company?
I asked for a coffee break.

Why did you give up playing the accordion?
I always pinched my stomach.

Why did you hit your wife with a chair?
I couldn't lift the table.

Why did you leave New York?
I couldn't bring it with me.

Why did you throw out your alarm clock?
It always went off when I was asleep.

Why did you put your toupee in your tuba?
I wanted to blow my top.

Why do they call him wonder boy?
They look at him and wonder.

Why do you always carry a compass?
So I'll know whether I'm coming or going.

Why do you carry that cane?
Because it can't walk.

Why do you eat your dessert first?
My stomach is upset.

Why do you follow the truck in front of us?
I have to. He is towing us.

Why do you have a statue under the sink?
Shh! That's the plumber.

Your car really runs smoothly.
Wait, I didn't start the motor yet.

You're wearing one red and one green sock!
I know. And I even have another pair just like that at home.

You've never heard of the Ten Commandments? What's your name?
Moses.

Why do you keep hitting your head?
I'm trying to break up this cold.

Why do you keep looking down all the time?
My doctor told me to watch my stomach.

Why do you put your foot on the stove?
I want to pop my corn.

Why do you sing with your eyes closed?
I hate to see people suffer?

Why do you want sixty pennies?
I thought a little change would do me good.

Why does your dog keep turning around in circles?
He is a watchdog and he is winding himself up.

Why does your dog sleep on the stove?
He wants to be a hot dog.

Why the large handkerchief?
For crying out loud!

Why this small glass of whiskey?
Didn't you ask for a shrimp cocktail?

Wilt thou take this woman as thy lawful wife?
I wilt.

Who's never hungry at the Thanksgiving dinner?
The turkey—he's stuffed!

Who is that man with the purple thumb?
That's Joe. The near-sighted carpenter.

Would you like to see a model home?
Glad to. What time does she quit work?

You didn't eat your breakfast, dear.
No, I can't eat on an empty stomach.

You have your shoes on the wrong feet.
But these are the only feet I have.

You look very tired.
Sure I am. For days I've been trying to throw away my boomerang.

You say you smoke five packs a day. Doesn't it make you sick?
Why should it? I only smoke the packs not the cigarettes.

You told me you had no mosquitoes in your hotel.
They aren't ours. They come from the other hotels.

Three-Liners

A noise woke me up this morning.
What was it?
The crack of dawn.

Answer the phone.
But it's not ringing.
Why wait until the last minute?

Are you a giant fan?
Yes.
Well, I'm a little air conditioner.

At the movie last night all of a sudden everybody got up and walked out.
Why, what happened?
Nothing, the picture was over.

Can I borrow $10 till payday?
When is payday?
I don't know, you're the one that's working.

Dad, give me a dime.
You're too old to be begging for dimes.
Okay, give me a dollar.

Did you ever see me before in your life?
No.
Then how do you know it's me?

Did you hear that all buses stop in New York?
Why?
To let the people off.

Did you hear what the burglar gave his wife for her birthday?
No.
A stole.

Did you say that your dog's bark was worse than his bite?
Sure, I did.
Well, don't let him bark. He just bit me!

Do you hear something?
No.
That's funny. I'm talking to you.

Do you know what time it is?
Sure, I do.
Thanks.

Do you know who stays up all night.
No.
The Statue of Liberty.

Do you make those jokes up yourself?
Out of my head.
You must be.

Doc, I have carrots growing out of my ears.
How did it happen?
I don't know. I planted cabbage.

Doctor, I've had a dime stuck in my ear for months.
Why didn't you come to me sooner?
I didn't need the money.

Doctor, I keep thinking I'm a bridge.
What's come over you?
Four cars, two trucks and five buses.

Doc, my son is always emptying ashtrays.
Oh, there's nothing wrong with that.
In his mouth?

For months I thought I was a dog, but my psychiatrist cured me.
How are you now?
Fine, feel my nose.

Fire Department? My house is on fire.
How do we get there?
Don't you have your red fire truck anymore?

Get me a shovel, fast! George is stuck in the mud up to his shoelaces.
Why doesn't he just walk out?
He went in head first.

Good news! I have saved up enough money for us to go to Europe.
When do we leave?
As soon as I have saved enough money for us to come back.

He's my best friend.
How long have you known him?
Since yesterday.

I bought you a beautiful surprise for your birthday.
Good, let's see it.
Wait till I put it on.

I cried at the movie last night.
Why, was it sad?
No, but I missed the price change by two minutes.

I drink ten cups of coffee a day.
Does it keep you awake?
It helps.

I expect some money from MGM.
MGM?
Yes, My Grand Mother.

I got my wife a lady's watch.
Did she like it?
Yes, but the lady came and took it back.

I just bought this emerald for my girl.
But an emerald is green.
Well, just wait'll she wears it awhile.

I just discovered an amazing device that sews buttons on clothes.
What is it?
A needle and thread.

I just had a swim in the ocean.
How did you find the water?
Gosh, you can't miss it.

I keep thinking I'm a dog, Doc.
How long has this been going on?
Since I was a little puppy.

I never use an umbrella when it rains.
So what do you do?
I just get wet.

I once had a dog that never ate meat.
How come?
We never gave him any.

I once had a parrot for five years and it never said a word.
It must have been tongue-tied.
No, it was stuffed.

I only drink to forget.
Forget what?
I don't remember.

I really have a problem getting along with people.
Why don't you see a psychiatrist?
I can't. I'm not allowed on the couch.

I still have bumps on my head from my tonsil operation.
How could you get bumps on your head from a tonsil operation?
They ran out of ether.

I take the worst possible view of everyone.
Oh, you're a pessimist.
No, a passport photographer.

I think I've kissed every doctor in this hospital.
Intern?
No, alphabetically.

I told you not to call me at work.
But, darling, the hall mirror broke.
Well, I'll look into it when I get home.

I already took 100 pictures with my new camera.
Where did you get all the film?
What film?

I was born in New York.
What part?
All of me.

I weigh a hundred and five pounds with my glasses.
Why include your glasses?
Because I can't read the bathroom scale without them.

I went bowling last night and liked it better than golf.
How come?
Well, I bowled all night and didn't lose a single ball.

I went to the movies yesterday and I had to change my seat several times.
Heavens! Did a man get fresh?
Finally.

I wish I had a sore eye.
Why?
You'd sure be a sight for it.

I wrote a book and it's going like wildfire.
Like wildfire?
Yes, everybody is burning it.

I'd like a ticket for the show.
You want a downstairs ticket for $5 or upstairs for $3?
What's playing upstairs?

I'd rather kiss my wife than eat.
Why? Because she's so attractive?
No, because she's such a bad cook.

If it weren't for the mustache, you'd look like my wife.
But I have no mustache.
I know, but my wife has.

I'll be a friend to you to the end.
That's great. Could you lend me $15?
That's the end.

I'll have you know I once wrote for the *New York Times*.
What happened?
They sent it to me.

I'd like some rat poison.
Will you take it with you?
No, I'll send the rats over for it.

I'll never forget the day I was born.
Why, what happened?
I cried like a baby.

I'm going out after dinner.
Oh, darling, what will I do without you?
The dishes.

I'm not feeling well today. I ate a dozen oysters last night.
What did they look like when you opened them?
Oh, you have to open them?

I'm very busy around the house. I wash the windows, wash the dishes.
What about your maid?
Oh, she washes herself.

Mom, I just knocked over the ladder in the garden.
You'd better tell your dad.
He knows; he was on the ladder at the time.

Mom, may I go out and play?
With this hole in your socks?
No, with the kids next door.

Mom, may I have ten cents for a man who's crying outside?
What is he crying about?
"Ice cream, 10 cents!"

Mommy, look! I can write!
What did you write?
I don't know, I can't read.

Mother, I broke a leg off the chair.
How did you do that?
I was pounding it with your new camera.

My boyfriend took me to a drive-in movie last night.
How was the movie?
What movie?

My brother can't work without liquor.
How come?
He's a bartender.

My brother is a conductor.
Railroad or musical?
Electrical. He was hit by lightning.

My brother is crazy. All day he goes around biting nails.
What's so bad about that?
He is a carpenter.

My doctor told me to drink carrot juice after a bath.
How does it taste?
I don't know, I'm still drinking the bath.

My father lost money on everything my brother made.
What did your brother make?
Mistakes.

My friend goes to bed with his shoes on.
Who's that?
My horse.

My friend has snew in his blood.
What's snew?
Not much. What's snew with you.

My girl friend is a twin.
How do you tell them apart?
Her brother is taller.

My mother got a black eye last night.
She should put a piece of steak on it.
If we'd had steak in the house, my father wouldn't have hit her.

My name is XQNGRYZ.
Are you Polish?
No, I'm an optician.

My sister put our Venetian Blinds into the washing machine by mistake.
So what happened?
Do you know anybody who can use eighty thousand toothpicks?

My sister was overcome by heat.
In this cool weather?
Yes, she fell in the furnace.

My uncle was punished for taking pictures.
How come?
He took them out of the museum.

My wife had an argument with the electric company.
Who won?
It's a tie. We don't get any electricity and they don't get any money.

My wife just hired a new secretary.
Blonde or brunette?
Bald.

My wife just ran away with my best friend.
Who's your best friend?
The guy who ran away with her.

My wife left me and I want her back.
Because your heart is full of love?
No, the sink is full of dishes.

My wife was arrested for parking.
For parking?
Yes, for parking one car on top of the other.

Officer, I want to report a missing parrot.
Did he talk?
I hope not.

Pardon me, do you know the way to the bank?
No, I'm afraid not.
Well, it's two blocks on your right.

Please give a poor blind man a dime.
But you can see out of one eye.
Than make it a nickel.

Radio will never replace the newspapers.
How come?
You can't wrap packages with a radio.

Say, bartender, did I spend 100 dollars here last night?
Yes, you did.
Oh, that's good, I thought I had lost it.

Say, didn't I borrow $5 from you yesterday?
No.
How careless of me. Could you give it to me now?

Say, Grandpa, can you spit through your whiskers?
You bet, Sonny.
Better do it now. They're on fire.

Say, honey, could you fix my purse?
Sure, what's wrong?
It's empty.

Say, man, could you spare a dime?
No, but come along. I'll buy you some breakfast.
I don't want to. I've eaten three breakfasts already trying to get a dime.

Say, where is this train going?
This train goes to Florida in about twenty minutes.
Oh, that sure is a fast train.

Since I lost all my money, half of my friends won't talk to me.
How about the other half?
They didn't find out yet.

Sonny, don't blow up that paper bag.
Why not?
There are still some groceries in it.

They had to shoot poor old Fido.
Was he mad?
He wasn't too pleased.

This is a dogwood tree.
How can you tell?
By its bark.

Today is my wife's birthday.
What are you getting for her?
Make me an offer.

Waiter, bring me a 3 1/2.
What's that?
A half a bottle of *7 Up*.

We have a new bouncing baby in our house.
Boy or girl?
I don't know. It hasn't stopped bouncing yet.

Well, finally I got into the movies.
How did you do it?
I paid them $1.50.

What do you call frozen ink?
Iced ink.
You're telling me!

Where did you get that black eye?
You know that pretty women we said was a widow?
Now you found out she isn't.

Where does a dog go when he loses his tail?
Okay, where?
To a retail store.

Where were you born?
In a hospital.
Oh, what was the matter with you?

Where were you last New Year's Eve?
I don't remember anymore.
That's too bad. You should have been with me. I had a good time.

Why are you looking into the mirror?
I'm looking for new wrinkles.
What's wrong with the old ones?

Silly Jokes

Two-Liners

Am I the first girl you ever kissed?
It's quite possible. Were you in Atlantic City, in 1959?

Are you allergic?
No, I'm Harry.

Are you home sick?
No, I'm here sick.

Are you musically inclined?
Oh, yes. At the age of two I started to play on the linoleum.

Are you unattached?
No. I'm just sloppily put together.

At college, did you sleep in a dormitory?
No, in my pajamas.

Before I take this job, tell me, are the hours long?
No, only sixty minutes.

Can I put this wallpaper on myself?
Sure, lady, but it will look better on the wall.

Can I sell you a vacuum cleaner?
No, we have no vacuum to clean.

Can you do anything other people can't?
Sure. I can read my own handwriting.

Can you read Chinese?
Only when it is printed in English.

Could you give a poor fellow a bite?
I don't bite myself, but I'll call the dog.

Daddy, give me a nickel to buy some ice cream.
Oh, keep quiet and drink your beer.

Did someone take your pulse?
No, nurse, I still have it.

Did you ever take your girl through the tunnel of love?
No, I'm afraid of the dark.

Did you know it takes five sheep to make a sweater?
I didn't even know they could knit.

Did you meet your son at the station?
Oh, no, I've known him for years.

Did you seal the letter with a kiss?
No, with rubber cement.

Did you turn on the light in the entrance?
I don't know. It was too dark out to see.

Do ships sink very often?
Only once.

Do these stairs take you to the second floor?
No, you'll have to walk.

Do you believe in Buddha?
Why, of course, but I think margarine is just as good.

Do you believe in clubs for women?
Only in self-defense.

Do you ever feel your liquor?
No, why should I get my fingers wet?

Do you ever gamble?
I was married three times.

Do you have animal crackers?
No, but I have some nice dog biscuits.

Do you know Lincoln's Gettysburg Address?
No, I didn't even know he had moved.

Do you know what a vacuum is?
It must be dirty because they have so many cleaners for it.

Do you say a prayer before you eat?
No, we don't have to. My mother is a good cook.

Do you want your pizza sliced into eight pieces?
Better make it six, I don't think I can eat eight pieces.

Doc, what can I do about my broken leg?
Limp.

Doctor, every bone in my body hurts.
Be glad you're not a herring.

Doctor, there's an invisible man in your waiting room.
Tell him I can't see him right now.

Does a window pane?
No, but a kitchen sinks.

Does your dog have a license?
Heavens, no! I do all the driving.

Does your dog have any fleas?
Silly. Dogs don't have fleas. They have puppies.

Don't walk so far now. Take the bus home.
No use. My wife won't let me keep it in the house.

Every time you have a few drinks you start to recite poetry.
Don't you know that two pints make one quote?

Golf is sure a stupid game.
You are so right! I'm glad I don't have to play until tomorrow.

Have any big men been born in this town?
No, only little babies.

Have you anything snappy in rubber bands?
No, but we have something catchy in fly paper.

Have you filled the salt shaker yet?
Not yet. I'm having trouble getting the salt through the little holes.

Have you got something in your eye?
No, I'm just trying to look through my finger.

Have you read *Webster's Dictionary?*
No, I'll wait until they make a movie out of it.

Haven't you heard of the fall of Rome?
No, but I remember hearing something drop.

Hey, Noah, wanna drink?
Noah don't!

Hey, what are you doing? Put down that gun!
Well, you told me to kill the motor.

How can you be so stupid and live so long?
I take good care of myself.

How can you make anti-freeze?
Hide her pajamas.

How come it takes you so long to cook that chicken?
Well, the cookbook says to cook one half hour to the pound and I weigh 110 lbs.

How to do you avoid a hangover?
Keep drinking.

How do you do?
How do I do what?

How do you feel about biting dogs?
I don't know, I've never bitten any.

How is your headache?
Out playing bridge.

How is your husband getting along with his golf?
Much better. The children are now allowed to watch him.

I'm going to put the cat out.
Why? Is it on fire?

I believe it's going to rain.
Yes, there is so much atmosphere in the air.

I can't marry you. You're practically penniless.
That's nothing. The czar of Russia was Nicholas.

I don't know the meaning of fear.
Why don't you look it up in the dictionary?

I have a pain in my left foot.
Try walking on the other foot.

I just bought a new set of balloon tires.
Oh, I didn't know you had a balloon.

I just saw a steam shovel.
Don't tell me! Nobody can shovel steam.

I'd like to propose a little toast.
Nothing doing! I must have a regular meal.

I lost twenty pounds while I was in England.
How much is that in American money?

I made up my mind to kiss every girl who says "How interesting!"
How interesting!

I met a man just now I haven't seen in twenty years.
That's nothing. I met a man I never saw before in my life.

I must charge you for murder.
All right. What do I owe you?

I never take anything lying down.
Not even a nap?

I ordered strawberry shortcake. Where are the strawberries?
That's what we are short of.

I saw you and your husband playing marbles on the lawn.
We weren't playing marbles. We had an argument and I was helping him pick up
his teeth.

I see they're adding a new wing to the new hospital.
They'll never get it off the ground.

I see you drink constantly.
No, I only drink beer.

I want some light coffee.
They all weigh the same.

I want to return this cottage cheese. It has a splinter in it.
What do you want for 50 cents? A whole cottage?

Is your house warm?
It should be. The painter put on two coats last week.

Is your steak tough?
And how! So far I have only bent the gravy.

Is your toaster a pop-up?
No, it's an Indian model. It sends up smoke signals.

Let me see your credentials.
I never wear them in the summertime.

Look, here is a green snake.
Leave it alone. It's probably just as dangerous as a ripe one.

Ma, the garbage man is here.
Tell him to leave three cans.

My wife is a medium.
That's nothing. My wife is a large.

My wife gave me a muffler for Christmas.
Oh, I didn't know you had a car.

Mother, may I watch the solar eclipse?
Okay, but don't go too near.

My daughter is going to play Beethoven tonight.
I hope she wins.

My son is a kleptomaniac.
That's wonderful! Where is his office?

Our tests show you are a kleptomaniac.
What can I take for it, Doc?

Say, honey, there are two flies in the kitchen.
That's too bad. We're not allowed pets in the apartment.

Say, how far is it to the Empire State Building?
Well, if you walk that way it's about 4,000 miles, but if you turn around it's right behind you.

Say, is it correct to eat chicken with your fingers?
No, you eat the chicken first, then you eat the fingers.

Say, this boat leaks.
Only on the end. We'll just sit on the other end.

Say, waiter, where is your menu?
The second door from the left.

Say, what time is it?
I don't know, I'm a stranger in this town.

Say, your house is burning.
That's O.K. I have enough lumber in the attic to build a new one.

So, you're an alien?
No, I'm feeling fine.

So, your uncle fell down all those stairs.
Yes, but it was all right; he had to come down anyway.

Stick out your tongue!
Why? I'm not mad at you, doctor!

Those, madame, are our satin pants.
Yes, I see. Now bring me a pair that wasn't sat in.

There's a button in my salad.
I suppose it fell off while the salad was dressing.

This is a dangerous world we live in.
Yes, very few get out alive.

Waiter, what's good to eat?
Candy bars, but they will spoil your appetite.

We're going to give the bride a shower.
Count me in. I'll bring the soap.

What can I do for you?
I want a pair of glasses that make me look taller.

What did you buy those nails for?
For ten cents.

What do you know about Eskimos?
I eat their pies.

What do you think of Red China?
Oh, it looks good on a white tablecloth.

What's wrong with this chicken, nothing but skin and bones?
Well, what do you want, feathers?

What should I do about a loud car squeak?
Play your car radio louder.

When will you straighten out the house, dear?
Why, is it tilted?

When your baby starts crying at night, who gets up?
Everybody in the building.

Where can one get a drink, day or night?
At Sing Sing, that place is full of bars.

Where does a sheep get his hair cut?
At a ba-ba shop.

While I was out, did you take any messages?
No, sir. Are there any missing?

While we were hunting, I spotted a leopard.
I thought they came that way.

Why are you eating so fast?
I'm afraid I might lose my appetite before I'm finished.

Why are you jumping up and down?
I took some medicine and forgot to shake well before using.

Why are you standing at this corner?
The cop told me to catch the 14th Street bus and only 10 have passed so far.

Why are you standing in front of the mirror with your eyes closed?
To see what I look like when I'm asleep.

Why are you eating your ice cream so fast?
My mother just called me for lunch.

Why do you have a pickle behind your ear?
Oh, I must have eaten my pencil for lunch.

Why do you have so many sleeves on your coat?
Why? That's my coat of arms.

Why do you keep scratching yourself?
I'm the only one who knows where it itches.

Why do you play so much golf?
My doctor said I must take my iron every day.

Why do you wear empty eyeglass frames?
The lenses hurt my eyes so I took them out.

Why does your wife always wear a flower in her hair?
She wants to show who wears the plants in the family.

Why don't you drink tea anymore?
A teabag got stuck in my throat once.

Why don't you soak your feet in hot water?
What? And get my shoes wet?

Would you buy a ticket? We're holding a raffle for a poor old lady.
Why would I want to win a poor old lady?

Would you like your coffee black?
What other colors do you have?

Would you shoot a horse with a wooden leg?
No, I'd shoot him with a gun.

You have the Asian flu.
But, doctor, I've never been to Asia.

You know, my little son has been walking for four months!
Really? Isn't it time he sat down?

You must buy a ticket to go in.
But my name is John Crime and crime doesn't pay!

You must have a good excuse for the black eye.
No, if I had a good excuse my wife wouldn't have given it to me.

You want to work here. Can you shoe horses?
No, but I can shoo flies.

You're really ignorant.
Thanks, and I thought all the time I was stupid.

Your food gives me heartburn.
What did you expect, sunburn?

Your umbrella looks as though it's seen better days.
It *has* had its ups and downs.

Three-Liners

All my husband does is hunt and drink.
What is he hunting?
Something to drink.

Can you draw a straight line with a ruler?
Of course.
That's odd. I use a pencil.

Did you ever tickle a mule?
No, I haven't.
Try it. You'll get a kick out of it.

Did you know there was a kidnapping down the street?
No, what happened?
His mother woke him up.

Did you lose your wallet?
No.
Then lend me ten dollars.

Did you misplace your glasses?
Why do you ask?
Because you drink from the bottle.

Do you have any talcum powder in this drugstore?
Yes, just walk this way.
If I could walk this way, I wouldn't need the talcum powder.

Do you have time for a couple of dillies?
Sure, why not.
O.K. Dilly, Dilly.

Do you know how to drive a baby buggy?
No.
Just tickle its feet.

Do you know that England is farther away than the moon?
How come?
I can see the moon but I can't see England.

Do you know where elephants are found?
No, where are they found?
They are so big, they're seldom lost.

Do you want to see something swell?
Yes.
Put a sponge in water.

Doc, is it normal to fall in love with an octopus?
No.
Well, do you know anybody who would buy eight engagement rings?

Doc, will I be able to read with those glasses?
You sure will.
That's great. I never could read before.

Every night I dream that I'm flying.
Why don't you sleep on your back?
What? And fly upside down?

Give me a round-trip ticket.
Where to?
Back here, of course.

Have you seen the evening paper?
No, what's in it?
My lunch.

Hello, is this the fire department?
Yes, lady, can we help you?
Please tell me, where is the nearest fire box? I want to report a fire!

Help! An alligator bit off my leg.
Which one?
I don't know. All these alligators look alike.

Help! I can't swim.
Why not?
I'm not in the water.

Hey, put this box to your ear and listen.
I don't hear a thing.
I know. It's been like that all day.

Honey, there's water in the carburetor.
Where is the car?
In the lake.

How much is five Q and 5 Q?
Ten Q.
You're welcome.

How do you feel?
I can't kick.
Rheumatism, eh?

How do you top a car?
I don't know.
Top on the brake, tupid.

How is your new girl?
Not so good.
You were always lucky.

I always see spots before my eyes.
Didn't the new glasses help?
Sure, now I see the spots much clearer.

I can bend bars with my bare hands.
Iron bars?
No, chocolate bars.

I crossed a movie with a swimming pool.
What did you get?
A dive-in theater.

I could marry a girl with $100,000.
Why don't you?
I don't have $100,000.

I don't like this chair; it's too small.
But it's a Louis the Fourteenth.
It's still too small. Maybe you have a Louis the Fifteenth?

I dreamed last night that someone stole my clock.
And when you woke up it was gone?
No, but it was still going.

I dropped my watch in the river and it's still running.
What? The watch?
No, the river!

I gave my husband a big surprise on his birthday.
What did you give him?
Breakfast!

I have a fine apartment for you.
By the week or by the month?
By the incinerator.

I have a maid problem. They are hard to hold.
Why?
They are so ticklish.

I have an unusual dog. He has no nose.
How does he smell?
Awful.

I have no windshield on my car.
How do you keep the wind from hitting your face?
I ride the bus.

I haven't slept for days.
Aren't you tired?
No, I sleep nights.

I heard something this morning that opened my eyes.
What was it?
My alarm clock.

I just finished this puzzle.
Did you do it in a jiffy?
No, in the living room.

I keep seeing spots before my eyes.
Have you ever seen a doctor?
No, only spots.

I keep thinking that today is Monday.
But today is Monday.
I know. That's why I keep thinking it is.

I know something that will tickle you.
What is it?
A feather.

I know what you are going to say next.
What?
That's what!

I like bowling. I'd rather bowl than eat.
Doesn't your wife object?
No, she'd rather play bridge than cook.

I love to sit in bed and ring the maid.
I didn't know you had a maid.
I don't, but I have a bell.

I once drove from New York to Bermuda.
That's impossible. There's an ocean between.
No wonder I had to use my windshield wiper all the time.

I once wrote myself a letter.
What did you say?
I don't know, I never got it.

I put one over on the railroad today.
How?
I bought a return ticket and I'm not coming back.

I saw something last night that I shall never get over.
What was that?
The moon.

I see my friend gave you a black eye.
But you don't even know that man.
Well, he's my friend now.

I tried many banks today but couldn't get what I wanted.
What did you want?
Credit.

I used to have freckles but no more.
What did you do?
I washed the mirror.

I want to speak to Mr. Dill.
Is it B as in Bill?
No, D as in pickle.

I was born in Chicago.
Before the fire?
No, behind the piano.

I was in a taxi with my girl last night and snuggled up very close.
How far did you go?
Just two blocks. I had only one dollar.

I was in plenty of hot water last night.
What happened?
I took a bath.

I weighed only two pounds when I was born.
Only two pounds? Did you live?
Did I? You should see me now.

I would like to buy a nice easy chair for my husband.
Morris?
No, Freddy.

If I send a letter airmail will it be in Miami tomorrow?
Yes.
That's funny, it's addressed to Chicago.

I'm celebrating my wife's fifth anniversary.
Wedding anniversary?
No, fifth anniversary of her 30th birthday.

I'm a little worried about my brother.
Why?
He wants to beat his drum—from the inside.

I'm only 27 years old.
Indeed?
No, in June.

Is a chicken big enough to eat when it's two weeks old?
Of course not.
Then how does it stay alive?

Is it correct to say you water the horse?
Yes, dear.
Then I'm going to milk the cat.

Is your refrigerator running?
Yes, it is.
Better catch it before it gets away.

I've lost my little dog.
Why don't you put an ad in the paper?
Silly, my dog can't read!

I've often been compared to Gable.
Who made the comparison?
My wife, she seems to prefer Gable.

I've lost quite a lot of weight.
I don't see it.
Sure you don't! I've lost it.

Lend me ten dollars until I come back from Chicago.
When are you coming back?
Who's going?

Let's play Building and Loan.
How do you play that?
You get out of the building and leave me alone.

Look, there's a henweigh on your neck.
What's a henweigh?
Oh, about three pounds.

My coat feels black.
You can't feel color.
Why, didn't you ever feel blue?

Oh, today I played awful, I even lost a ball.
Don't worry, many people lose golfballs once in a while.
But I was bowling!

Please run upstairs and get my watch.
Maybe it will run down.
No, it won't, we have a winding staircase.

Say, conductor, where do I have to transfer?
Where are you going?
That's none of your business.

Say, look in the mirror quick, what do you see?
Why? That's me.
Thanks. I thought it was me.

Say, stewardess, how high is the plane?
About 30,000 feet.
I see, and how wide is it?

Some men took away my car.
Did you notify the police?
They're the ones who took it.

The other day I was looking for a book, and all of a sudden I stopped.
Why?
I found it.

There are two things I can't eat for breakfast.
What are they?
Lunch and dinner.

There's something wrong with those sponges.
Why?
They're full of holes.

They now have a gadget that allows you to see through walls.
What do they call it?
A window.

They now have a special flight to Mexico for $50.
But I paid $200.
Yes, but you flew inside the plane.

This match won't light.
What's the matter with it?
I don't know, it just lit before.

This morning I fell over forty feet.
Did you get hurt?
No, but I had an awful time getting off that bus.

Waiter, bring me a ham sandwich.
With pleasure.
No, with mustard.

Waiter, where does this coffee come from?
Brazil, sir.
No wonder it's cold!

Wanna fly?
Sure do.
I'll catch one for you.

Want to hear a couple of lulus?
Sure.
Lulu, lulu.

Want to see something swell?
Sure.
Hit your finger with a hammer.

What are you doing to those chickens?
Dressing them.
What! You have to dress and undress them everyday?

What are those holes in the board?
They're knot holes.
Well, if they are not holes, what are they?

What did you have for dinner?
Three guesses.
No wonder you're hungry.

What's the date today?
Look at your newspaper.
But that's yesterday's paper.

What's the difference between an elephant and a matterbaby?
What's a matterbaby?
Nothing, what's the matter with you?

When does eleven plus two equal one?
I don't know.
On a watch.

Where do you bathe?
In the spring.
I said, where not when.

Who was Snow White's brother?
Who?
Egg white. Get the yolk?

Will you buy this book from me?
No, we only buy whole libraries.
But this is my whole library.

You can take the finger off the leak now.
Thank Heavens! Is the plumber here yet?
No, the house is on fire.

You hammer like lightning.
You mean I'm fast?
No, I mean you seldom strike the same place twice.

You know, I used to ride in my own carriage.
When was that?
When I was a baby.

You know that piano stool you sold me?
Yes?
Well, I turned it in all directions and can't get a single tone out.

You need glasses.
But I'm wearing glasses, Doctor.
Then I need glasses.

You'd better keep your eyes open tomorrow morning.
Why?
You might fall down the stairs.

You look like a million dollars.
But you have never seen a million dollars.
That's what I mean. You look like something I have never seen before.

Are you positive?
Only fools are positive.
Are you sure?
I'm positive.

Do you realize you were driving down a one-way street?
But I was only driving one way.
Didn't you see the arrows?
I didn't even see the Indians.

We had a big fight about the way we should celebrate our silver wedding anniversary.
That's too bad. How long are you married now?
Two years.

What is the name of your dog?
Ginger.
Does Ginger bite?
No, Ginger snaps.

Cruel Jokes

Two-Liners

All that I am, I owe my mother.
Why don't you send her 50 cents and pay up the bill?

But, why honey, did you buy me such a small diamond?
I didn't want the glare to hurt your beautiful eyes.

Come now, Freddy, and kiss your aunt.
Why Ma? I didn't do anything.

Darling, do you realize this is our anniversary?
Please—not while I'm eating!

Did you ever see anyone like my wife?
Yes, once, but I had to pay admission.

Do you think getting drunk is the best way to celebrate our anniversary?
Who's celebrating?

Do you want red or white wine with our supper, honey?
Neither. With your cooking all I need is a stomach pump.

Doctor, could you remove my double chin?
Only a guillotine could ever do that!

Excuse me for living.
All right. But don't let it happen again.

Give me a kiss before supper.
What? And spoil my appetite?

How are we going to celebrate our anniversary, honey?
How about five minutes of silence.

How do you like my biscuits?
Good. Did you buy them yourself?

How is your wife?
Expensive.

How many dead people are in this cemetery?
All of them.

I brought a friend home for dinner?
Who wants to eat friends?

I cook and bake for you and what do I get? Nothing!
You're lucky. I get indigestion.

I don't like the way you're holding the gun.
Well, I don't aim to please.

I hate to tell you this, but your wife fell into the well.
That's okay. We never drink that water anyhow.

I once had a mustache like yours, but it looked so bad I cut if off.
I had a face like yours but it looked so bad I got a mustache.

I saw your new scarecrow on your farm.
That's not a scarecrow. That's my aunt Sally.

I want some rat poison.
Should I wrap it up or do you want to eat it right here?

I wish I had a nickel for every boy who asked me to marry him.
What would you do? Buy a pack of gum?

I wonder why my girl keeps closing her eyes whenever I kiss her.
Did you look in a mirror lately?

I'm getting divorced.
Who's the lucky man?

I'm giving a dinner for all my friends tonight.
Oh, did you reserve a table for two?

I've been drinking all my life and it never ruined my appearance.
No? Have you any idea what did it?

If you don't stop drinking, I'm going to leave you.
I'll drink to that.

Is it painful to be a moron?
It must be. You look awful sad.

Is your wife the quiet, refined type?
No, she is still living.

It's our fifth anniversary and you look just the same as at our wedding.
I should. I'm still wearing the same dress.

Ma, Dad was hit by a car!
Don't make me laugh, son.

Ma, why do I always walk in circles?
Keep quiet or I'll nail your other shoe to the floor.

May I have the next dance?
Sure, I don't want it.

Mom, Daddy just fell off the roof.
I know, dear. I saw him pass the window.

Mom, when will we get a garbage can?
Shut up and keep eating.

My brother has a wide aquaintance.
Yes, isn't she?

My meatballs will melt in your mouth in seconds.
Sure, but they usually stay in my stomach for weeks.

Nobody cares if I drink myself to death.
I do. You are using my liquor.

Now why did you shoot your husband with a bow and arrow?
I didn't want to wake the children.

Of course I know "The Road to Mandalay."
Then why don't you take it?

Officer, there's a man following me. I think he's drunk.
Yes, he must be.

Pardon me for dancing on your feet.
Oh, that's all right. I dance on them myself.

Say the word that will make me happy the rest of my life.
Get lost!

Say, you shouldn't hit a man when he's down.
What do you think I got him down for?

Wanna make me happy?
No, why should I drop dead?

Waiter, this soup tastes watery.
Wait till you taste our coffee.

Was she embarrassed when you asked her to take off the mask?
She sure was. She wasn't wearing any.

What are you mourning for?
My wife's first husband.

What, 15 dollars for just a small bag of groceries?
You want it in a bigger bag?

What would I have to give you for a kiss?
Chloroform.

Why did they put a fence around the graveyard?
Because so many people are dying to get in.

Why do you always close your eyes when you dance with me?
I hate to see my feet suffer.

Why don't you cook like my mother?
All right. I'll cook like your mother. I'll burn everything.

Would you like to dance the next one?
Sure. If you find a partner for me.

You have been an awfully dull wife.
Just give me a chance and see what a fine widow I'll make.

You mean to say that physical wreck gave you a black eye?
He wasn't a physical wreck until he gave me the black eye.

You've got the brain of an idiot.
You want it back?

Your sister is spoiled, isn't she?
No, that's just the perfume she's wearing.

Three-Liners

Broke my kid of biting nails.
Really? How?
Knocked his teeth out.

Did anyone ever take you for a human being?
Lots of times.
Well, people will make mistakes.

Every time I go to the movie, some fat lady munches popcorn next to me.
Why don't you change seats?
I can't. It's my wife.

How do you feel?
I feel like I look.
That's too bad.

I always do my hardest work before breakfast.
What is that?
Getting up.

I thought of you all day yesterday.
How nice. Where have you been?
At the zoo.

I want some arsenic for my wife.
Have you a prescription?
No, but here is a picture of her.

I would cry if you died.
Show me how much.
Die first.

I'm going to visit Yellowstone Park.
Don't forget Old Faithful.
Oh no. I'm taking her with me.

Mom, Daddy is being chased by a bull.
What can I do about it?
Put some film into the camera, fast!

My alarm clock woke me this morning for the first time.
How come?
My wife hit me on the head with it.

My best friend just ran away with my wife.
Was he handsome?
I don't know. I never met the fellow.

My mother went down to buy a revolver.
Did your father tell her what to get?
No, he doesn't even know she's going to shoot him.

My second wife is even.
Even what?
Even worse than my first wife.

The man who was run over by a car is now out of danger.
That's good.
Yes, he died this morning.

This operation will cost you 400 dollars.
Can you do it for 200, doctor?
Sure, but I'll have to use duller knives.

Was there ever a suicide in your family?
No, there never was.
Then why don't you break the monotony?

Want to lose some ugly fat?
Sure.
Then cut off your head.

Who is that terrible looking woman over there?
That's my sister.
Of course. I didn't notice the resemblance.

Would you walk ten miles because you love me?
I certainly would.
Good. Because you just missed your last bus.

Why don't you go back to the old country?
What old country?
Any old country!

You must be 44 years old.
How did you know?
My brother is 22 and he's half nuts.

You sure have a grouch here.
That's not a grouch, that's a duck.
I know. I was talking to the duck.

Witty Dialogues

Two-Liners

HE—SHE

HE: Would you marry an idiot for his money?
SHE: Is this a survey or a proposal?

HE: So he broke your heart?
SHE: Not only that. He played with father and broke him, too.

HE: I'm going to ask some girl to marry me. What do you think of it?
SHE: It's a fine idea, if you ask me!

HE: Every time I put on a clean shirt, some buttons are missing. What should I do?
SHE: Either get married or get divorced.

HE: You don't know how nervous I was when I proposed to you.
SHE: And you don't know how nervous I was until you did.

HE: You only married me for my money.
SHE: Well, I couldn't get it any other way.

HE: May I see you pretty soon?
SHE: Don't you think I'm pretty now?

HE: So you told Charlie you loved him after all?
SHE: I didn't want to, but he squeezed it out of me.

HE: When did your parents get married?
SHE: I don't know. It must have been before I was born.

HE: I would get on my knees and die for you.
SHE: Would you stand on your feet and work for me?

HE: Why won't you marry me? Is there someone else?
SHE: There must be.

HE: Will you marry me?
SHE: No, but I will always admire your taste.

HE: I would like to meet a girl who doesn't flirt, giggle, gossip, smoke, drink, pet and kiss.
SHE: Why?

HE: Do you like a big wedding or little ones?
SHE: I'd rather have the big wedding first.

HE: I can't face any more bills.
SHE: Don't face them, foot them!

HE: I love you so much I could die for you.
SHE: Why don't you?

HE: I love you, I adore you. Will you kiss me?
SHE: What for?

HE: I got a pearl out of an oyster.
SHE: I got a diamond out of an old nut.

HE: Will you join me in a cup of tea?
SHE: Will there be room for both of us?

HE: Are you trying to make a monkey out of me?
SHE: No, nature took its own course.

HE: I want to see you in the worst way.
SHE: Come around before breakfast.

HE: Ours is a puppy love.
SHE: That's why you treat me like a dog?

HE: I have a cold in my head.
SHE: That's better than nothing.

HE: You know, I have the cutest apartment.
SHE: Well, let's not get into that.

HE: I had a nightmare last night.
SHE: Yes, I *saw* you with her.

HE: Someday, darling, I shall die and leave you.
SHE: How much?

HE: I suppose you think I'm a perfect idiot.
SHE: Oh, none of us is perfect.

HE: Darling, may I kiss your hand?
SHE: Sure, but don't burn your nose on my cigarette.

HE: May I join you, Madame?
SHE: Heavens! Am I coming apart?

HE: I'm not as dumb as I look.
SHE: You *couldn't* be.

HE: You look like a million.
SHE: But I'm only 23!

HE: I wish I had been born in the dark ages.
SHE: So do I. You look terrible in the light!

HE: Tell me, what would go best with my new tie?
SHE: A beard.

HE: This fellow is the ugliest person I ever saw.
SHE: Not so loud. You forget yourself.

HE: Pardon me, but you look like Helen Green.
SHE: So what? I look worse in pink.

HE: Would you care if I left you?
SHE: Not if you left me enough.

HE: Thanks for the dance.
SHE: The pressure was all mine.

HE: What would you do if you could play the piano like me?
SHE: Take more lessons.

HE: Your wish is my command.
SHE: Get lost.

HE: I would like to have some old-fashioned loving.
SHE: Come to my house and I'll introduce you to my grandma.

HE: (over the phone) Where can I get hold of you on Tuesday?
SHE: I don't know. I'm kind of ticklish.

HE: Aren't you ready yet?
SHE: I've been telling you for the last hour that I would be ready in a minute!

HE: I keep hearing the word *idiot*. I hope you're not referring to me?
SHE: Don't be so conceited, as if there were no other idiots in the world.

HE: When you go to the park, why don't you take one of the children along?
SHE: Why not? Which one do you think would go best with my new dress?

HE: For the last time I'm telling you, I wasn't out gambling with the boys last night.
SHE: Then how come you just shuffled the toast and dealt me five slices?

HE: There are two men I really admire.
SHE: Who is the other?

HE: I used to think ...
SHE: What made you stop?

HE: My boss said I was a young man who would go far.
SHE: You're going just so far—no matter what your boss said.

HE: I wish you would stop buying so many things on credit.
SHE: But, dear, it only proves that I have confidence in you.

HE: I would die for you.
HE: How soon?

HE: So he is teaching you how to swim. What did you learn so far?
SHE: That he's 25, single and has a good job.

HE: Just think, we've been married twenty-four hours.
SHE: Yes, it seems like it was only yesterday.

HE: I saw Tim today and he didn't even greet me. He probably thinks I'm not his equal.
SHE: Why that stupid, brainless, conceited moron. You are certainly his equal.

HE: That's a flimsy dress you're wearing.
SHE: That's a flimsy excuse for staring.

HE: I bought you a Rembrandt and a Rolls-Royce; did they arrive yet?
SHE: Yes, they arrived—but tell me which is which.

HE: I have the physique of a boy of twenty.
SHE: You better give it back to him. You're getting it out of shape.

HE: I'll be seeing you.
SHE: Please don't threaten me!

HE: You're always wishing for something you haven't got.
SHE: Well, what else can one wish for?

HE: I know I proposed to you last night but I can't remember whether you accepted or not.

SHE: I knew I said "no" to somebody last night but couldn't remember to whom.

HE: We're coming to a tunnel. Are you afraid?

SHE: Not if you take that cigar out of your mouth.

HE: Tonight you dance with me, and I suppose tomorrow you'll be making a date with some other man.

SHE: Yes, with a chiropractor.

HE: Would you be angry if I proposed?

SHE: It depends on what you propose.

HE: If you refuse me, I will never love another.

SHE: Yes, but what if I accept you?

HE: I wonder if I could make you melt in my arms.

SHE: No, I'm not that soft and you're not that hot.

HE: What is the idea telling everybody I'm stupid?

SHE: Oh, I didn't know it was a secret.

HE: I wish I had a nickel for every girl I kissed.

SHE: What would you do? Buy a package of chewing gum?

HE: I'm going to kiss you before you go.

SHE: Why don't you do it while I'm still young?

HE: Take me in your arms and press my lips.

SHE: Why? Are they wrinkled?

HE: You had no right to kiss me that way.

SHE: All right. I'll try another way.

HE: Love makes the world go round.

SHE: So does a couple of martinis.

SHE—HE

SHE: Tell me what you eat and I'll tell you what you are.

HE: Waiter, cancel my order of shrimps!

SHE: Oh, dear, I'm always forgetting.

HE: So I notice; you're always out for getting this or for getting that.

SHE: Well, I have decided to marry that struggling young actor.

HE: If you have decided, he may as well stop struggling.

SHE: Every handsome fellow I've met is conceited.

HE: Oh, I don't know—I'm not.

SHE: Do you think I look old?
HE: No, indeed; you're not half as old as you look.

SHE: I want an explanation and I want the truth.
HE: Make up your mind. You can't have both.

SHE: How did you break your engagement to Sally?
HE: I just told her my salary.

SHE: Be careful with this vase. It's 300 years old.
HE: Don't worry. I'll treat it as if it were new.

SHE: You always used to say I have a body like a beautiful ship.
HE: Yes, but since then your cargo has shifted.

SHE: I thought Freddy was a friend of yours.
HE: He used to be until he introduced me to my wife.

SHE: Oh, John, when we were first married you used to tickle my chin; do it again.
HE: Which one?

SHE: What caused the big explosion in your house last night?
HE: It was touched off by a little powder on my collar.

SHE: Meet me at the corner at eight tonight.
HE: Fine, and what time will you be there?

SHE: Did you ever see me before?
HE: Sure, before, behind and sideways.

SHE: Darling, will you love me when I'm old?
HE: Of course, I do.

SHE: Say something soft and sweet to me.
HE: Custard pie.

SHE: My age? Oh, I just turned 23.
HE: Oh, I see, 32!

SHE: I have just reached 27.
HE: What delayed you?

SHE: I'll be ready in a minute, dear.
HE: There's no hurry now. I have to shave again.

SHE: Honey, today we are married twelve months.
HE: It seems more like a year to me.

SHE: Where did you learn to kiss like that?
HE: I'm a glassblower.

SHE: Where did you learn to kiss like that?
HE: Drinking at slow water fountains.

SHE: Where did you learn to kiss like that?
HE: I used to blow up footballs.

SHE: Do you wear nightgowns or pajamas?
HE: No.

SHE: Tell me that you love me.
HE: Please, not while I'm eating!

SHE: I'm going home to mother.
HE: That's better than her coming here.

SHE: Did you hear that mouse squeaking?
HE: What do you want me to do? Oil it?

SHE: I can read my husband like a book.
HE: Then be careful and stick to your own library.

SHE: Did she give you her hand after you kissed her?
HE: Yes, right across my mouth.

SHE: So your wife went to Europe for her health. What did she have?
HE: Eight hundred dollars her father gave her.

SHE: Do you realize that you talk in your sleep?
HE: And you begrudge me those few words?

SHE: Oh, he's so romantic. He always calls me "Fair Lady."
HE: Force of habit. He's a conductor.

SHE: Before we were married you used to catch me in your arms.
HE: Now I catch you in my pockets.

SHE: I really believe he married her only because he wanted a good housekeeper.
HE: And now I suppose he wishes he could give her a month's notice.

SHE: I have something to confess to you, now that we are married: I can't cook.
HE: Well, don't worry, I write poetry for a living. There won't be much to cook.

SHE: I can't give you another dance, but I'll introduce you to the prettiest girl here.
HE: I don't want to dance with a pretty girl, I want to dance with you.

SHE: The captain asked me to sit on his right hand tonight for dinner.
HE: What's he gonna stir his coffee with?

SHE: When you yawn, put your hand to your mouth.
HE: What? And get bitten?

SHE: How can I keep my husband from looking at other women?
HE: Give him some poison to drink.

SHE: Will you buy me an ice cream sundae?
HE: I don't think I will be here Sunday.

SHE: Is it your ambition to leave footprints on the sand of time?
HE: Not just now. I'm trying to cover up my tracks.

SHE: Are you satisfied with married life?
HE: Yes, I'm satisfied—I've had all I want of it!

SHE: Why do you call your new home your "Dream House"?
HE: Because it cost me twice as much as I dreamed of.

SHE: Do you really think I'm a thing of beauty?
HE: Yes, honey, and I'd like to be your joy forever!

SHE: I'm going home to my mother.
HE: Good. I'll come with you. Then we'll both get a decent meal.

SHE: Why do you insist on marrying a rich girl?
HE: So I can give her everything her money can buy.

SHE: Would you come and help me in distress?
HE: Sure, I wouldn't care what you were wearing.

SHE: I can't decide whether to go to a palmist or to a mind reader.
HE: Go to a palmist; you *do* have a palm.

SHE: That handsome man kissed me last night and today the whole town knows it.
HE: Goodness, how did you spread the news so quickly?

SHE: Tell me that you love me.
HE: Okay, but don't ask me to write it down.

SHE: Why do you always go out with two girls?
HE: In case of a flat tire it's nice to have a spare.

SHE: What would you rather give up—wine or women?
HE: It depends on the vintage.

SHE: My husband is the only man who ever kissed me.
HE: Are you bragging or complaining?

Three-Liners

HE: I'll grant you your smallest wish.
SHE: Do you really mean that?
HE: Sure, dear, if it's small enough.

HE: I lost my gold fountain pen.
SHE: You should have had a string on it.
HE: I did. And I lost that, too.

HE: When I was five years old my Dad took me to the zoo.
SHE: What happened?
HE: They refused me.

HE: It will take me a long time to forget you.
SHE: How long?
HE: Beg your pardon—have we met?

HE: That was a good job I had. I used to get two dollars a day when it didn't rain.
SHE: What did you get when it rained.
HE: Wet.

HE: I came in on a radio train.
SHE: A radio train?
HE: Yes, it stopped every five minutes for station announcements.

HE: I took my girl to the movie and she screamed twice.
SHE: Twice?
HE: Yes, once at the movie and once at me.

HE: When I hitchhike I never take a ride until I ask the driver his name.
SHE: Why do you do that?
HE: I don't ride with strangers.

HE: In my class I was a moron.
SHE: Was that good?
HE: In *my* class, it was.

HE: It's impossible to make a woman happy.
SHE: Just give her all the money she could spend.
HE: I just said it was impossible.

HE: Some girls are bad, but you're an exception.
SHE: Thank you.
HE: Yes, exceptionally bad.

HE: I'm reading a mystery story.
SHE: But that's our budget ...
HE: I know.

HE: I took my girl to the tunnel of love yesterday.
SHE: Gee, what happened?
HE: I don't know. We couldn't get a seat together.

HE: How about having dinner with me?
SHE: Sorry, you're not my type.
HE: All I want is a date, not a blood transfusion.

HE: May I have the next dance?
SHE: Sorry, but I'm engaged.
HE: Well, I don't want to marry you—I just want to dance.

SHE: You would be a fine dancer except for two things.
HE: What's that?
SHE: Your feet.

SHE: A man tried to kiss me last night.
HE: Did you slap his face?
SHE: Yes, as soon as he got through.

SHE: Wouldn't you be surprised if I gave you a check for your birthday?
HE: I sure would.
SHE: Well, here it is, all made out. Ready for you to sign.

SHE: If you're not careful you're going to have trouble with the brunette over there.
HE: That's my wife. What makes you say I'm going to have trouble with her?
SHE: There's a blonde hair on your coat.

SHE: I always had a soft spot in my heart for you.
HE: Then let's get married.
SHE: I said soft spot in my heart, not in my head!

SHE: You know, I'm 5 ft. 6 in. stripped.
HE: But you don't have to strip to have your height read.
SHE: That's what I told the doctor.

SHE: Will you marry me?
HE: No, I won't.
SHE: Oh, come on, be a support.

SHE: Do you have a good memory for faces?
HE: Of course, I have.
SHE: Good. I just broke your shaving mirror.

SHE: Do you want to start the TV?
HE: Why do you ask?
SHE: It's about time you started something.

SHE: Bob told me I was the eighth wonder of the world.
HE: What did you say?
SHE: I told him not to let me catch him with any of the other seven.

SHE: I'm just crazy to get married.
HE: Then marry me.
SHE: I'm not that crazy.

SHE: You remind me of an ocean.
HE: Wild, romantic and restless?
SHE: No, you make me sick.

SHE: She sure gave you a dirty look.
HE: Who?
SHE: Mother Nature.

Did you hear about ...

One-Liners

... the accordion player who made his living by playing both ends against the middle?

... the accountant who kept hearing strange invoices?

... the actress who went with every Tom, Dick and Harry to get an Oscar?

... the aging actress who had her jewelry, her driver's license and her face lifted the same day?

... the ambitious band leader who hired more musicians than he could shake a stick at?

... the ambitious bathing beauty who had trouble getting into the social swim?

... The army dog who got a tree-day pass?

... the army dog who wanted to be transferred to a new post?

... the auto mechanic who went to a psychiatrist and from force of habit climbed under the couch?

... the ballplayer who was trying to get to first base with an old bat?

... the bandit who walked into an insurance office and escaped without buying any?

... the bank teller who thought he didn't count for much?

... the beatnik who became rich and hired a chauffeur for his motorcycle?

... the bedbug who had a baby in the spring?

... the blind man who picked up a hammer and saw?

... the boy scout who did so many good turns, he got dizzy?

... the boy who had high blonde pressure?

... the boy who dreamed he ate 30 pounds of marshmallows and when he woke up his pillow was missing?

... the bride who was so ugly everybody kissed the bridesmaid?

... the burglar who became so rich, he stopped making housecalls?

... the bus that was so crowded that even the bus driver had to move to the rear?

... the cab driver who had such a bad day, his flag was at half mast?

... the cannibal who went to a psychiatrist because he was fed up with people.

... the captain who got sore because someone sent him a letter marked "Private"?

... the carpenter who caught his foot on the roofing and came down with the shingles?

... the carpenter who drove a nail through his thumb and now has a thumbnail?

... the ceiling who said to the wall "Hold me up boys, I'm plastered"?

... the chicken farmer who was henpecked?

... the child from Texas who walked up to Santa Claus and asked "What can I do for you?"

... the child who looked all over for the Easter eggs until he found out his mother had scrambled them?

... the chimney sweep who lost his balance and came down with the flue?

... the conceited starlet who has unlisted measurements?

... the conceited plumber who took one look at Niagara Falls and said, "Give me time and I could fix it"?

... the conductor who couldn't face the music?

... the cop who gave out 22 parking tickets before he discovered he was in a drive-in movie?

... the couple who had such a miserable vacation they didn't even bother to have their film developed?

... the couple who saved up all winter for a summer vacation—last summer's?

... the couple who separated because she had a winning smile but he was a bad loser?

... the dentist who married a manicurist and they've been fighting tooth and nail ever since?

... the disagreeable guy who had his phone installed just so he could hang up on people?

... the distillery that pays time and a fifth for overtime?

... the drive-in movie that ran out of film and nobody knew the difference?

... the drycleaner who worked on the same spot for four years?

... the dumb crook who held up a bunch of tourists on their way home from Las Vegas?

... the dumb girl who turned a deaf ear to a blind date?

... the economy flight where they show home movies made by the pilot?

... the electrician who gave all his friends shorts for Christmas?

... the elephant who complained, "I'm getting sick and tired working for peanuts"?

... the Eskimo whose wife left him cold?

... the farmer who ran a steam roller over his field because he wanted to raise mashed potatoes?

... the father who fainted when his son asked for the garage key and came out with the lawn mower?

... the fellow who became a chain smoker because he couldn't afford cigarettes?

... the fellow who crossed an intersection with a convertible and got a blonde?

... the fellow who fell into the lens grinder and made a spectacle of himself?

... the fellow who had his nose lifted and now he smells to high heaven?

... the fellow who heard so much about the birds and bees he couldn't get interested in girls?

... the fellow who lost a looking glass in the woods and went crazy combing the brush for the mirror?

... the fellow who put on a clean pair of socks every morning but at the end of the week he couldn't get his shoes on?

... the fellow who saw flying saucers after he pinched a waitress.

... the fellow who spent five hours trying to get the English Channel on television?

... the fellow who spent so much money on his girl, he had to marry her for his money?

... the fellow who threw away his socks because they weren't worth a darn?

... the fellow who was so dumb that the fortune teller read his mind for half the price?

... the fellow who was so henpecked he was afraid to ask his wife for a new apron?

... the florist who closed his shop on Mother's Day?

... the gambler who found that trying to beat the law was a bad bet?

... the ghost who was so shy he couldn't even spook for himself?

... the girl who graduated from cooking school with flying crullers?

... the girl who had a complexion like a peach—yellow and fuzzy?

... the girl who learned to ski in just ten sittings?

... the girl who thinks a mushroom is a place to love?

... the girl who was so pleased with her wedding that she could hardly wait for the next one?

... the girl who wore a mini-skirt out in the rain and it shrank something wonderful?

... the golfer who cheated so much that when he got a hole in one he put down zero on his score card?

... the go-go dancer who couldn't shake off a cold?

... the guy who got a tow truck and now works as a bouncer in a drive-in theater?

... the guy who robbed a music store and escaped with the lute?

... the hairdresser in Arizona who dyed with his boots on?

... the head nurse who married a foot doctor?

... the Hollywood star who wanted to get divorced in the same dress in which her mother got divorced?

... the husband who helped his wife into the car when he was sure nobody was looking?

... the husband who shot a lifeguard for giving his wife mouth-to-mouth resuscitation, six months after he saved her?

... the husband who sent his wife to the Thousand Islands and told her to spend a week on each?

... the hypochondriac who had a birthday and all the guests brought germs?

... the hypochondriac who was so neurotic that he took an overseas shot before he went to see a foreign movie?

... the jockey who felt his employer should stop horsing around?

... the karate expert who stuck out his hand to make a left turn and cut a car in half.

... the college boy who was too lazy to write home for money?

... the little country girl who always went out with city fellows because farm hands are too rough?

... the little strawberry who was worried because his parents were in a jam?

... the magician who once walked down the street and turned into a bank?

... the mailman who cut a big hole into his mailsack because the mail must go through?

... the man who bought a pair of tight shoes when he found a box of corn plasters?

... the man who called his stockbroker for a loan and found out the stockbroker was broker than he was?

... the man who had a waterproof, shockproof, unbreakable, anti-magnetic watch and lost it?

... the man who had no respect for age unless it was bottled?

... the man who had such big feet, he had to put his pants on over his head?

... the man who opened a fortune cookie in a Chinese restaurant and found a note from his wife telling him to come home, supper is ready?

... the man who ordered a yard of pork and got three pig's feet?

... the man who wanted to get a charge out of life, so he studied electricity?

... the man who wanted to get a flue shot but his bartender didn't know how to mix one?

... the man who was lucky in love—until his wife heard about it?

... the man whose ambition is to have as much money as his wife thinks he has?

... the manicurist who married a chiropodist, and now they wait on each other hand and foot?

... the mattress tester who was fired for not laying down on the job?

... the mint-flavored shoes for government officials who keep putting their feet in their mouths?

... the musician who worked all week on an arrangement, and then his wife didn't go out of town after all?

... the nearsighted glow worm who fell in love with a cigarette?

... the nearsighted snake who fell in love with a rope?

... the new all-filter cigarettes for people who light the wrong end anyway.

... the new fire department that doesn't make house calls?

... the newlywed couple who almost starved to death because the husband hid the can opener?

... the nudist who kept feeling hot and cold all over?

... the old lady who got some wheels for her rocking chair so she could rock and roll?

... the owl who didn't give a hoot?

... the photographer who was handed a negative by his girl?

... the pilot who was afraid to fly?

... the plumber who made no house calls?

... the preacher who complained that he was working himself to death for Heaven's sake?

... the psychiatrist who gave his son a set of mental blocks for Christmas?

... the publisher who told the author, "Your novel is excellent, but right now we are looking for trash"?

... the Pullman porter who just wrote a book titled, *Berth Control*?

... the pussycat who ate a ball of wool and had mittens?

... the rare medium who always orders her steak medium rare?

... the religious moth who gave up woolens for lint?

... the rich Texan who is going to buy a country home as soon as he decides which country?

... the rich Texan whose parrot said, "Polly wants a cracker with caviar on it"?

... the seasick man who put glue in his soup to keep it down?

... the singer who could hold a note longer than the Bank of America?

... the snake who gave birth to a bouncing baby boa?

... the steer who when he saw the branding iron said, "This looks like a hot number"?

... the swanky hotel where they air-conditioned the steam room?

... the tattoed sailer who went around with a ship on his shoulder?

... the taxi driver who was troubled with a hacking cough?

... the telephone operator in Chinatown who keeps getting wong numbers?

... the termite who walked up to a bar and asked, "Is the bar-tender here?"

... the two rabbits who got married and went on a bunnymoon?

... the umbrella manufacturer who saved his money for a rainy day?

... the undertaker who advertised in *Life*?

... the unlucky prospector who went out West to hunt uranium and all he kept finding was gold?

... the woman who bought a gown for a ridiculous price, while her husband thought she got it for an absurd figure?

... the wristwatch without numerals on the dial for people who don't care what time it is?

... the young lover who took it for granite when his wife made him a marble cake?

Did you hear about ...

Two-Liners

... Abraham Lincoln having bad eyes?
    He never got a driver's license.

... the account executive who lost a million-dollar account?
    His hair turned charcoal-gray overnight.

... the astronaut who gave up being rocketed into space?
    His wife wouldn't let him travel alone.

... the cannibal who was on a diet?
He ate only midgets.

... the cannibal who was expelled from school?
He was caught buttering up the teacher.

... the Charles Dickens martini?
No olive or twist.

... the comic who told the same jokes three nights running?
He wouldn't dare tell them standing still.

... the cow that got a divorce?
Someone gave her a bum steer.

... the cowardly counterfeiter?
He still has the first dollar he ever made.

... the crook who forgot himself?
He went out and stole his own car.

... the doctor who did magic?
A man swallowed a nickel, and he made him cough up five dollars.

... the dog with cauliflower ears?
He's a boxer, but not a very good one.

... the efficiency expert who overdid it?
He put unbreakable glass in all the fire alarms.

... the Egyptian girl who didn't know right from wrong?
Now she's a mummy.

... the fellow who brushed his teeth with gunpowder?
Now he's shooting off his mouth all day.

... the fellow who got a dog for his wife?
I'd like to make a swap like that myself.

... the fellow who stirred his mush with his fingers?
He wanted to feel his oats.

... the fire at the shoe factory?
Ten thousand soles were lost.

... the ghost who hasn't been working for a month?
His sheets got lost in the laundry.

... the girl who's looking for a guy with a strong will?
Made out to her, of course.

... the girl who was allergic to mink?
She gets sick every time she sees one on another girl.

... the glass blower who inhaled?
Now he has a pane in his stomach?

... the guy who didn't enjoy his stay in Las Vegas?
The weather was hot and the dice were cold.

... the henpecked husband who hasn't spoken to his wife in months?
But he feels his turn is due soon.

... the Indians who opened a bar on Broadway?
They sell Manhattans for $24.

... the jury that couldn't convict the defendant?
It didn't want to get involved.

... the little boy whose home ran away from him?
He lived in a trailer.

... the magician who turned photographer?
But his hocus-pocus was out of focus.

... the man who just came back from a pleasure trip?
He took his mother-in-law to the airport.

... the man who was too lazy to walk in his sleep?
He hitchhiked.

... the marriage of the two shoes?
It didn't work out too well—she was a sneaker and he was a loafer.

... the nearsighted man from Texas?
He bought the Pacific Ocean thinking it was a large swimming pool.

... the new airplane our Air Force has developed?
It goes faster than money.

... the new credit card for wives?
It self-destructs after $100.

... the new perfume with a secret ingredient?
It makes a man think he can support a wife.

... the new see-food diet?
You can see food, but you can't touch it.

... the new tombstone for cigarette smokers?
It's a silly millimeter long.

... the old lady who was 90 years old and didn't need glasses?
She drank straight from the bottle.

... the pilot who joined the nudist colony?
He couldn't take off anymore.

... the rock-and-roll singer who retired?
His voice was okay, but his legs were gone.

... the sailor who had 26 wives?
He really wasn't a sailor—he was a whole-sailer.

... the sales manager who only hired married men?
He figured they were used to taking orders.

... the student who discovered a way to play hookey from correspondence school?
He sent in empty envelopes.

... the tough boss?
He was raised on marble cake, rock candy, and brick ice cream.

... the very brave traffic light?
It refused to turn yellow.

... the violinist's wife who couldn't get any sleep?
His fiddling kept waking her up.

... the woman who was at an awkward age?
She no longer remembered how old she was.

... the wrestler who couldn't understand that he lost the bout?
He won the rehearsal.

Did you hear the joke about ...

Three-Liners

... the bad pudding?
No.
You wouldn't swallow it.

... the bed?
No.
No wonder. It isn't made up yet.

... the beauty contest?
No.
You wouldn't get it anyhow.

... the blotter?
No.
It's very absorbing.

... the bomb?
No.
Oh, drop it!

... the broken pencil?
No.
There's no point to it.

... the bumblebee?
No.
It just flew away.

... the butter?
No.
I won't tell it. You might spread it.

... the cards?
No.
No deal.

... the ceiling?
No.
I didn't think so. It's over your head.

... the chocolate pie?
No.
It's rich.

... the cigar?
No.
It went up in smoke.

... the clock?
No.
Tick tock, tick tock.

... the coffee?
No.
Oh, it's hot stuff.

... the dirty shirt?
No.
That's one on you.

....the dirty window?
No.
You wouldn't be able to see through it.

... the door?
No.
It's closed now.

. . . the express train?
No.
Oh, you just missed it.

. . . the fight on the train?
No.
The conductor punched a ticket.

. . . the fire?
No.
It's a hot one.

. . . the fly?
No.
You will never catch it.

. . . the hot potato?
No.
Let's just drop it.

. . . the leaking bag?
No.
Then it hasn't leaked out yet.

. . . the lunch box?
No.
All baloney.

. . . the memory course?
No.
Oh, now I forgot it.

. . . the mountain?
No.
It's a big bluff.

. . . the mousetrap?
No.
It's pretty snappy.

. . . the mule?
No.
You'll get a kick out of it.

. . . the new hairdo?
No.
Just keep it under your hat.

. . . the new swan song?
No.
That's swan on you.

... the old battery?
No.
It's no good anymore.

... the oyster?
No.
It's too raw.

... the peacock?
No.
It's a beautiful tale.

... the pretty knife?   .
No.
It's sure sharp.

... the pushcart?
No. How does it go?
It doesn't. You have to push it.

... the Q-Tip?
No.
There's something for your ear.

... the rope?
No.
Oh, skip it!

... the sugar in the coffee?
No.
It dissolved.

... the three He men?
No.
He, He, He.

... the three holes in the ground?
No.
Well, well, well.

... the trap?
No.
Oh, spring it.

... the traffic light?
No.
Oh, it just turned yellow.

... the tunnel?
No.
Oh, you wouldn't dig it anyhow.

... the wall?
No.
It's all cracked.

... the well?
No.
It's too deep for you.

I Heard

I heard Bill was the life of the party.
That's right. He was the only one who could talk louder than the radio.

I heard every time your husband goes fishing he brings something home.
That's right. Usually a sunburn and poison ivy.

I heard Jim works now as a baker.
I guess he kneads the dough.

I heard mosquitos bother you only three times a day.
That's right. Morning, noon and night.

I heard mustard can give you a heart attack. That's ridiculous.
Yeah? Just try and get some on your new suit.

I heard so much about you.
You'll have an awful time proving anything.

I heard that Jack kissed you last night.
He did not. Besides, he promised not to tell.

I heard that kissing spreads disease.
Let's start an epidemic.

I heard that Lisa had a runaway marriage.
Yes, the groom took one look at her and ran away.

I heard that Mrs. Jones is down with blood poisoning.
That old gossip! She must have bitten her own tongue.

I heard that Rudolph is getting married next week.
Good, I never liked the fellow.

I heard the tree surgeon had an accident.
Yes, he fell out of his patient.

I heard they will never hang a man with a wooden leg.
I know. They use a rope.

I heard you applied for a government job. What are you doing now?
Nothing. I got the job.

I heard you are a good hairdresser. What do you have for grey hair?
The greatest respect, madame.

I heard you are a musician.
No, but I play the saxophone.

I heard you are going to move.
Yes, from area code 106 to 207.

I heard you are now selling furniture for a living. Any success?
So far I have only sold my own.

I heard you are secretly married to Alice.
No, she knows all about it.

I heard you are singing at weddings. What do you usually sing?
Soprano.

I heard you became a big movie star. Are you married?
Occasionally.

I heard you bought a bar for your den.
Yes, a candy bar.

I heard you bought some period furniture.
Yes, they went to pieces in a short period.

I heard you bought some wash-and-wear pants.
Yes, I wash them and my wife wears them.

I heard you bought three lawn mowers.
I had to; I have two neighbors.

I heard you broke up with that doctor you were going with.
Yeah, not only did he ask for his ring back, he sent me a bill for 32 house calls.

I heard you cancelled your life insurance.
Yes, I got tired of my wife telling everybody that I was worth more dead than alive.

I heard you don't drink anymore.
I don't drink any less, either.

I heard you don't read music.
No, you see one note, you've seen them all.

I heard you dropped a hundred pounds.
Yes, I dropped my girl friend.

I heard you only eat little food.
That's right, because big food gets stuck in my throat.

I heard you go to work everyday in a taxi.
Yes, I'm a cab driver.

I heard you got a new dish washer.
Yes, I got married again.

I heard you got beat up kissing the bride.
Yes, because it was two years after the wedding.

I heard you got some knick-knacks.
Yes, I got some nicks in my neck.

I heard you had a big fire at your house.
Yes, my wife lit all the candles on her birthday cake.

I heard you had twins.
Yes, but first I thought the doctor was giving me a choice.

I heard you have a cat that can say her own name.
Yes, meow.

I heard you have dinner out with your wife twice a week.
Yes, she goes on Tuesday and I go on Friday.

I heard you have a terrible disposition.
Yes, and I have to take her with me wherever I go.

I heard you made a lot of money in the stock market.
Yes, I bought Seven-Up when it was only six-and-one-half.

I heard you made two pictures in Hollywood.
Yes, one from the front and one from the side.

I heard you met your wife in the garden.
Yes, I was a dead beat and she was an old tomato.

I heard you missed school yesterday.
Not a bit.

I heard you play golf. What's your handicap?
A wife and two children.

I heard you played your trumpet all night.
That's right and at three in the morning my neighbor kept knocking on the walls
for an encore.

I heard you sent your daughter to a finishing school.
Yes, we felt it was either her finish or ours.

I heard you taught your wife how to play bridge.
Yes, and last week I won back my salary.

I heard you took an aptitude test.
That's right. And they found out I'm best suited for retirement.

I heard you took the Smith twins out yesterday. Did you have a good time?
Yes and no.

I heard you went nonstop cross-country. Why?
I couldn't find a parking space.

I heard you were arrested for stealing a watch.
That's right. The lawyer got the case and the judge gave me the works.

I heard you were engaged to a promising young lawyer.
Yes, but he didn't keep his promise.

I heard you will move to Chicago, permanently.
No, not permanently, Illinois.

I heard you work as a sword swallower.
Yes, that's my bread and butter now.

I heard your boyfriend is an electrician.
Yes, he's alternating between me and the girl next door.

I heard your brother died a natural death.
Yes, he was hit by a car.

I heard your dentist charges five dollars for a cavity.
That's right. You pay him five dollars and you get one.

I heard your doctor has a new shock treatment.
Sure, he sends you the bill in advance.

I heard your friend had an accident.
Yes, he got tired waiting for the elevator and went down the shaft without one.

I heard your friend had a finger in a big transportation deal.
Yes, he thumbed a ride across the country.

I heard your girl gave you back your ring.
Yes, she mailed it back marked, *Glass, handle with care!*

I heard your girl is a toe dancer.
And how, she dances all over my toes.

I heard your girl wants to become a singer.
That's right, but I think her voice is only good for cooling soup.

I heard your husband is in the hospital. What happened?
Knee trouble, I found a blonde on it.

I heard your sister got married. Who's the lucky man?
My father.

I heard your TV set brought you a lot of pleasure this summer.
Yes, I swapped it for an air conditioner.

I heard your new play is playing to standing room only.
Yes, nobody will buy a seat.

I heard your wife bought an estate in Reno.
Yes, it's only to have grounds for divorce.

I heard your wife bought a pressure cooker.
That's right, now I eat my supper from the ceiling.

I heard your wife came from a large family.
Yes, unfortunately she brought them with her.

I heard your wife can't cook.
That's right. And when I bought her a cookbook I found out she couldn't read either.

I heard your wife had her face lifted.
Yes, but it didn't take. When the doctor gave her the bill, it fell again.

I heard your wife has an hour-glass figure.
She *had*, until the sand shifted.

I heard your wife is a wonderful judge of men.
Yes, she can tell a man from a woman every time.

I heard your wife is expecting again.
Yes, she's expecting a new coat, a new car, and a new ring.

I heard your wife is on an onion diet. Did she lose anything?
Yes, five pounds and four friends.

I heard your wife isn't talking to you.
Yes, and all I did was sprinkle some tenderizer on her biscuits.

I heard your wife just bought a crazy dress.
Yes, and it fits her personality.

I heard your wife kept her girlish figure.
Kept it? She doubled it!

I heard your wife ran away with your best friend.
Yes, and am I going to miss him!

I heard your wife wants only the little things in life.
Yes, a little money, a little real estate, a little house.

 **3**

Insults

Crushing Insults

A crumb like you should have stayed in bed.

A day away from you is like a month in the country.

A guy with your IQ should have a low voice, too.

All I want for Christmas is your two front teeth!

All right. You've seen your shadow. Now crawl back into your hole.

All that he has today he owes.

Any similarity between you and a human being is purely coincidental.

Anyone who takes you for a darn fool makes no mistake.

Are those your ears, or do you model for ping-pong paddles?

Are you always so stupid or is today a special occasion?

Are you as stupid as you look?

Aren't you glad now you didn't throw away your clothes ten years ago?

As a failure, you are a fantastic success.

As an outsider, what do you think of the human race?

As long as you're standing, would you mind walking out?

At least there's one good thing about your body. It isn't as ugly as your face.

Be it ever so homely, there's no face like yours.

Being with you is like sitting on an unmade bed.

Brains aren't everything. In fact, in your case they're nothing.

Careful now. Don't let your brain go to your head.

Close your mouth before someone puts an apple in it.

Could I sell you a ticket to nowhere?

Despite what anyone says, I still think they are right.

Did you get caught with your face in a pencil sharpener?

Did you get your head in a pet shop?

Did you notice that the only time he listens is when he talks?

Did you use gun powder on your face? It looks shot.

Did you wake up with a pain in the neck this morning, or are you still single?

Did your mother have any children that lived?

Did your parents ever ask you to run away from home?

Didn't I see you in a bottle of alcohol?

Didn't I see your face on a bottle of iodine?

Didn't I see you once before? Under a microscope?

Didn't they name a town after you: Marblehead, Pennsylvania?

Do tell me about yourself. I adore horror stories.

Do you believe in hate at first sight?

Do you have a chip on your shoulder, or is it just your head?

Do you know what I like about you? Nothing!

Do you mind if I have you X-rayed? I want to see what people see in you.

Do you talk in your sleep? You certainly talk in mine.

Does your undertaker know you got up?

Don't be ashamed of what you are. I'm not ashamed of what you are!

Don't be mad at him. What's the use of being ignorant if you can't show it.

Don't be so smart. You can be replaced by a human being!

Don't call me, I'll call you!

Don't feel bad. A lot of people have no talent.

Don't get insulted, but is your job devoted to spreading ignorance?

Don't go away mad, just go away!

Don't go yet. I want to forget you exactly as you were.

Don't leave yet. Later on we serve brain.

Don't look now, but I think your brain is out of focus.

Don't lose your head—it's the best part of your body.

Don't mind him—he has a soft heart and a head to match.

Don't mind him, he's just talking to show he's alive.

Don't pay any attention to him. Don't even ignore him.

Don't take him too seriously; he's studying to be an idiot.

Don't tell me you're ignorant! I know it.

Don't think it hasn't been pleasant to meet you—because it hasn't!

Don't think, you may sprain your brain.

Don't think your're a bargain because you are half off!

Don't you get tired of having yourself around?

Don't you love nature, despite what it did to you?

Don't you need a license to be that ugly?

Every time you open your mouth, your foot falls out.

Everybody knows you're stupid; why do they still say you're dumb?

Excuse me, please, my leg has gone to sleep. Mind if I join it?

Fellows like you don't grow on trees; they swing from them.

50,000 manholes in the city and you had to drop in here!

For a moment I didn't recognize you and believe me, I never spent a more enjoyable moment.

Get a load of that voice! What do you gargle with? Serutan?

Give me time. I'll find a way to ignore you.

Have you been crying? Your face is clean.

Have you considered traveling lately?

Have you ever been to a zoo? I mean as a visitor?

He has a brilliant career behind him.

He has a concrete mind—permanently set and all mixed up.

He has a developed mind, but he's never used it yet.

He has a mechanical mind but some of the screws are missing.

He has a mechanical mind. Too bad he forgot to wind it up this morning.

He has a mind like a steel trap—always closed.

He has a strange growth on his neck: his head.

He has all the charm of a wrong number.

He has an unlisted personality.

He has a brain but it hasn't reached his head yet.

He has all the warmth of a 40-watt bulb.

He has more crust than a pie factory.

He has gone around with more women than the revolving door at Macy's.

He has water on his brain and liquor on his mind.

He has music in his soul. Even his shoes squeak.

He has the first penny he ever made, and in the original piggy bank.

He is a big wheel. He's always running around in circles.

He is a man of rare gifts—hasn't given any in years.

He is a man of the world—and you know what sad shape the world is in.

He is a man who will go far—and nobody will miss him.

He is a marvelous dresser for a man who never buys new clothes.

He is a pain in the neck, and some people have even a lower opinion of him.

He is a person who is going places. And the sooner the better.

He is a student of music. Knows every bar within ten miles of here.

He is a very friendly guy. Shakes hands even with the doorknobs.

He is a wonderful guy if you happen to like bums.

He is always around—when he needs you.

He is always lost in thought—it's unfamiliar territory.

He is an arsonist, a swindler, a forger, and a maniac; but remember, nobody is perfect.

He is an early bird who never catches the worm.

He is dark and handsome. When it's dark, he's handsome.

He is having business troubles. Can't mind his own.

He is just like a summer cold. You can't get rid of him.

He is knock-kneed, cross-eyed, overweight, stupid, vulgar, arrogant, and has bad breath. And those are his good points.

He is known as a miracle comic. If he's funny, it's a miracle.

He is known as a small talk expert. If there's nothing to be said, he'll say it.

He is known as the VIB: Very Insisting Bore.

He is listed in *Who's Who?*—under "What's That?"

He is living proof that a man can live without a brain.

He is making a comeback. He is trying to rejoin the human race.

He is nasty, repulsive and offensive, and those are his good points.

He is not a bad fellow until you get to know him.

He is not exactly a sculptor, just a chiseler.

He is not in *Who's Who?* He's in *Who's He?*

He is so cautious, he burns the bridges in front of him.

He is so dull, he couldn't even entertain a doubt.

He is so henpecked, he still takes orders from his first wife.

He is so henpecked, the only time he opens his mouth is to ask his wife where the mop is.

He is so short, when it rains he's the last one to know.

He is sure clever. Always puts away his problems for a brainy day.

He is such a coward, he won't even punch a time clock.

He is sweet, unpresuming and polite: a real phony.

He is the only man who can fall asleep in the middle of a nap.

He is the kind of man who picks his friends to pieces.

He is the kind of man who will borrow your pot to cook your goose.

He is the kind of man who would eat a frankfurter on a hamburger roll.

He is the kind of man who would hide your teeth and then offer you corn on the cob.

He is the kind of man who would steal a dead fly from a blind spider.

He is the kind of man you'd use as a blue print to build an idiot.

He is the type who'll cut your throat behind your back.

He is the world's biggest coward.

He is very intellectual. He can bore you on any subject.

He is very smart. He has an I.Q.

Here's 20 cents. Call all your friends and bring back some change.

His father was an electrician and he was his first shock.

His idea of an exciting night is to turn up his electric blanket.

His life is so dull, he looks forward to a dental appointment.

His mind is in great shape. He rarely uses it.

His mind is so small, it would ruin your eyes trying to read it.

His mother should have thrown him away and kept the stork.

His trousers are shabby and worn, but they *do* cover a warm heart.

His wit is about as sharp as a dull toothache.

How can I miss you if you don't want to go away?

How can you look so clean and laugh so dirty?

How come you are here? I thought the zoo was closed at night?

How did you get here? Wiggle off the fish hook?

How did you get out? Did someone leave your cage open?

How many years did it take you to become so ignorant?

How much do you charge to cause a nervous breakdown?

How much do you charge to haunt a house?

How much refund do you expect to get on your head, now that it's empty?

How would you like a blood test with some old razor blades?

How would you like a cup of poisoned borscht?

How would you like it if I grabbed your legs and made a wish?

How would you like to be the first man kicked into the orbit?

How would you like to come up here and get a slap in the face?

How would you like to feel the way you look?

I am a human being. What are you?

I'm busy now; do you mind if I ignore you later?

I'm glad you came. I haven't had a dull moment since the last time I saw you.

I'm not hard of hearing, I'm just ignoring you!

I'm your best friend and I don't even like you!

I bet your mother has a loud bark.

I bought my suit in a blackout. What's your excuse?

I can't seem to remember your name, and please don't help me.

I can't talk to you right now; tell me, where will you be in ten years?

I could break you in half, but who would want two of you?

I could get something for your voice—like laryngitis.

I could heckle you back, but why should I talk to a dummy?

I could make a monkey out of you, but why should I take all the credit?

I could say nice things to you but I'd rather tell the truth.

I couldn't warm up to him if we were cremated together.

I *do* wish I'd known you when you were alive.

I don't even like the people you're trying to imitate.

I don't know how old you are, but you don't look it.

I don't know if history repeats itself, but you certainly do.

I don't know what makes you so stupid, but it really works.

I don't know what makes you tick but I hope it's a time bomb.

I don't know what you are, but whatever it is, I hope you're the only one.

I don't know where you are going, but I hope you'll be on your way soon.

I don't know who you are, and I'm sure everybody will agree with me.

I don't want you to turn the other cheek. It's just as ugly.

I expect you to go places—and the sooner the better.

I feel sorry for your mother. She had no children to speak of.

I hate to talk about him behind his back, but it's safer that way.

I have compiled a list of your faults. It comes in 10 volumes.

I have had a wonderful evening, but this wasn't it.

I have heard so much about you; what's *your* side of the story?

I've seen better looking dummies than you in Macy's window.

I've seen bodies but you are ridiculous!

I've seen people like you before, but I had to pay admission.

I haven't seen anything like you since I gave up drinking.

I heard you like to travel, so why don't you?

I hope, for your sake, you're not as ugly as you look.

I hope it will make you happy that I will name my first ulcer after you.

I hope some day you'll jump on your bike and discover too late that it has no seat.

I hope you will always stay as unfriendly and dull as you are.

I hope you will come to my party. There's always room for one bore.

I hope your wife eats crackers in bed.

I hope you're going too far—and I hope you stay there.

I just hope your children are just as dumb as you are.

I just wish you'd lose your temper. The one you've got is awful.

I know I talk like an idiot, but I have to talk that way so you can understand me.

I know you were born silly, but why did you have a relapse?

I know you're a self-made man; it's sure nice of you to take the blame.

I know you're cut out to be a genius, but who put the pieces together wrong?

I know you're not as stupid as you look. Nobody could be.

I like long walks; why don't you take one?

I like the way you dress. Who cares whether or not it's in style.

I like the way you wear your teeth parted in the middle.

I'd like to compliment you on your work—when will you start?

I'd like to hear you talk—it sounds so good when you stop.

I'd like to help you out, which way did you come in?

I'd like to kick you in the teeth, but why should I improve your looks?

I'd like to run into you again, when you're walking and I'm driving.

I like you because you have an open face: open for improvements.

I like you better the more I see you less.

I like you. People say I have no taste, but I like you.

I like your approach—now let's see how fast you can leave.

I like your clothes. They look awful but the body they hide looks even worse.

I like your outfit, but I didn't know they made polka-dot tuxedos!

I like your outfit. Who wears your *clean* shirts?

I like your suit, but aren't you a little bit early for Halloween?

I like your suit, but I don't think this style will ever come back.

I like your suit. Do you always wear torn ones?

I like your suit; it's lushy, like it was cut from an old sofa.

I like your wallpaper, but who is your decorator? A garbage collector?

I liked you very much when we met, but you talked me out of it.

I must say, you have a ready wit. Let me know when it's ready!

I need you like Custer needed another Indian.

I need you like Rembrandt needed number paintings.

I need you like Venice needs a street sprinkler.

I never met a man I didn't like until I met you.

I now bid you a welcome adieu.

I promise you, if you walk out now, we won't talk about you.

I sure enjoyed talking to you. My mind needed a rest.

I sure like your suit. Who shines it for you?

I think he's an idiot but I may be overestimating him.

I think the stork that delivered you made a crash landing.

I think you're great. But what do I know?

I think you're terrible, and that's only a hint.

I think your brain is out of focus.

I think your family tree needs trimming.

I thought you were fat and ugly but you're not. You're skinny and ugly.

I thought you were the main feature in the zoo this week!

I want nothing out of you but breathing, and very little of that.

I'll bet you're the only nut in town not covered with chocolate.

I'll buy you a funeral plot if you move right in.

I'll buy you a kitten; you could use a new puss.

I'll forgive you for being so stupid.

I'll have to go out and eat. I can't take you on an empty stomach.

I'll knock you so high up in the air, you'll starve coming down.

I'll never forget a face, but in your case I'll remember both of them.

I will never forget the first time we met, but I keep trying.

I wish I could look that good in cheap clothes.

I wish I had a hearing aid so I could turn you off.

I wish I were a carpenter so I could fix your wagon.

I wish you were a fire so I could put you out.

I wish you were a headache; then I could take an aspirin and you'd go away.

I wish you were a TV set so I could turn you off.

I wish you were an asset so I could liquidate you.

I wish you were as dumb as you are stupid.

I wish you were *somebody* so you could make a comeback.

I wonder how you'd look stuffed.

I would like to be a magician so I could make you disappear.

I would like to have a lock of your hair. I'm stuffing a mattress.

I would like to pat your back with an axe.

I would like to say I like you, but why should I lie?

I would like to say something nice about you, but I can't think of anything.

I would like to take back my introduction to you.

I wouldn't believe him if he swore he was lying.

I understand everything except what you're saying.

If anybody asks you if you're living, just tell him it's a matter of opinion.

If anybody ever offered you a penny for your thoughts, there would be an inflation.

If baloney were snow, you'd be a blizzard.

If beauty were intoxicating, you'd be a whiskey sour.

If he said what he thought, he would be speechless.

If his face is his fortune, he's badly in need of a loan.

If his face is his fortune, he's headed for bankruptcy.

If his face is his fortune, he'd never have to pay income tax.

If his IQ were any lower, he'd trip over it.

If I gave you a drum, would you beat it?

If I gave you a going-away present, would you?

If I had a face like yours, I'd sue my parents.

If I had a face like yours, I'd walk backwards.

If I had a lower IQ, I could enjoy your conversation.

If I had a suit like your face, all wrinkled, I'd have it pressed every day.

If I had your face, I would hire a pickpocket to lift it.

If I have offended you, I'll gladly repeat it.

If I ignore you, would you go away?

If I said anything to insult you, believe me, I tried my best.

If I said anything to offend you, let me know; I might like to use it again.

If I said anything to offend you, please believe me!

If I wished you a Merry Christmas, cancel it!

If I were in your shoes I would get a shine.

If it weren't for your stupidity, you'd have no personality at all!

If rain makes flowers beautiful, you need a flood!

If she ever had to eat her words, she'd put on 15 pounds.

If someone tells you that you look good, slug him!

If the good die young, you'll live forever.

If there's an idea in your head, it's in solitary confinement.

If they ever put a price on your head—take it!

If we give you a fine send-off, would you go away?

If you're not too busy for the next hour, I'd like to talk to you for a minute.

If you're so smart, why aren't you rich?

If you don't go away and leave me alone, I'll find someone else.

If you ever bite your tongue, you'll die of acid poisoning.

If you ever get a penny for your thoughts—give change.

If you ever have to live your life over again, don't do it!

If you ever lost your face, it would be an improvement!

If you ever need a friend, come to me and I'll tell you where to go.

If you ever need a friend, get a dog!

If you ever need a friend, try and find one.

If you ever need me, please hesitate to call!

If you give him a penny for his thoughts, you're overpaying him.

If you had your life to live over again, don't do it!

If you have a brain operation it would be minor surgery.

If you have a minute to spare, tell me all you know.

If you have anything else to do, go ahead and do it!

If you have anything else to do tonight, don't neglect it!

If you have friends like him, you don't need enemies.

If you have some place to go—*go!*

If you have to live your life over again, do it abroad!

If you keep that suit long enough, some day it might come back in style.

If you kill yourself you'd get the right man.

If you like that suit, keep wearing it, no matter what people say.

If you must know, I'm ignoring you!

If you should disappear suddenly, it couldn't happen to a nicer guy.

If you think of something to say, don't mention it.

If you think you're a wit, make sure you're not half right.

If you want to be different, why don't you act normal?

If you were alive, you'd be a very sick man.

If you were a telephone I'd rip you off the wall.

If you were the only girl in the world, I'd shoot myself.

If you would be struck by lightning, would anybody care?

If you would have been with Washington he would have double-crossed the Delaware.

If your mouth were any bigger you could talk into your ears.

In honor of his great success, they have torn down the house where he was born to make room for a vacant lot.

Is he funny? He couldn't cheer up a laughing hyena.

Is it true you once bit your tongue and got food poisoning?

Is that a new hairdo or did you just forget to comb it?

Is that a new tie or did you just spill some soup on your old one?

Is that your Adam's apple or did you swallow a yo-yo?

Is that your beard or do you shave a hairy tongue?

Is that your face or is today Halloween?

Is that your face or are you breaking it in for a bulldog?

Is that your face or are you wearing a gas mask?

Is that your face or did you forget to wash this morning?

Is that your nose or are you eating a banana?

Is your stomach as sour as your face?

It takes real talent to be as dumb as you are.

It was nice of you to come. When are you leaving?

It will be tough getting along without you, but just let me try.

Just tell me, when was the last time you committed suicide?

Just what is it that you see in you?

Keep talking. Some day you'll say something intelligent.

Let me help you find some brain for you.

Let's play house. You be the door and I'll slam you.

Look, just because you have a head like a hubcap doesn't mean you're a big wheel.

Many people know something about everything, but you know nothing about anything.

May I be the first to shake your neck?

May I have the pleasure of saying goodbye to you?

May we have the pleasure of your absence?

Maybe you haven't any enemies, but none of your friends like you.

My wife wants a vacuum cleaner for Christmas. Is your head available?

Next time you give your clothes away, stay in them.

Next time you pass my house—please pass my house.

Nipping him in the bud won't stop *this* blooming idiot.

Nobody is perfect but you really take advantage of it.

No wonder you fly off the handle; you've got a screw loose.

Now, here is a self-made bore.

Of course, I'm listening to you. Didn't you see me yawning?

Oh, this is your bride! I thought it was your grandmother.

Oh, what wonderful hair you have. I have a lavatory brush at home just like it.

Please breathe the other way. You're bleaching my hair.

Please call me up some day so I can hang up on you.

Please close your mouth so I can see who you are.

Please close your mouth. There's an awful draft in here.

Please could I have your head for my rock garden?

Please do me a favor; the next time you talk to me, keep quiet.

Please don't tell me your name. Let me hate you incognito.

Please don't you ever change. Just stay as stupid as you are.

Please go back in your bread, you crumb.

Please go home and tell your wife to shoot her husband.

Please, I'm not a tailor; go have your fit somewhere else.

Please keep smiling. People will wonder what you are up to.

Please keep talking. You'll think of something to say.

Please let me say goodbye till we never meet again!

Please let's agree. If you don't say anything I don't have to listen.

Please may I borrow your I.Q.? I'm going out with a moron tonight.

Please may we have the pleasure of you leaving?

Please meet me at the beach. I'll give you drowning lessons.

Please meet me later at the bottom of the pool.

Please, Mister. I call you Mister despite all the evidence against you.

Please sit down and rest your mind.

Please stay with me. I want to be alone.

Please tell me, are you molded or fabricated?

Please tell me, did your mother have any children?

Please tell me, how do you know so much about nothing?

Please tell me, in the pinball game of life, how does it feel to be a tilt?

Please tell me, is your family happy or do you still live at home?

Please tell me, is your name Beethoven? You look like you just finished a fifth.

Please tell me, must you talk while I'm eating?

Please tell me, what is it that you see in yourself?

Please tell me, you were born, weren't you?

Please, the next time you are in my neighborhood, just keep going.

Please, will somebody help him find his brain?

Please, would someone show him the elevator shaft?

Say, could I drop you off somewhere? Say the roof?

Say, you got it! I don't know what it is, but you got it.

She looks like an old, worn-out mop handle.

So what if I made a mistake? I'm human; don't you wish you were, too?

Some day you will be arrested for impersonating a human being.

Some day you will find yourself, and you're going to be disappointed.

Some girls have dishpan hands; she has a dishpan face.

Some people live and learn; you just live.

Some people say he's good; some say he's rotten. I'm neutral: I say he's good and rotten.

Sometimes I wonder why your mother opened the door when the stork brought you.

That's a nice haircut you got. Where'd you get it? In a pet shop?

That's what this country needs: less men like you!

That's sure a fine suit you're wearing. Didn't they have it in your size?

That mustache becomes you. It breaks up the monotony of your face.

The last time I saw you was in a nightmare.

The more I see you, the less I like you.

The more I think of you, the less I think of you.

The next time I run into you on the street, I hope I'm in my car.

The next time you applaud, put your head between your hands.

The next time you cook with gas, inhale some.

The next time you order a toupee, get one with brains.

The next time you take a bath don't fight the current.

The next time you wash your face, wring it!

The only person who loves you is you!

The only time he's on the level is when he's sleeping.

The only thing big about you is your phone number.

The only thing female about her is her name.

The only thing I don't like about you is your face.

The only thing I like about him is his wife.

The only thing I like about you is your departure.

The only thing I like to say to you is goodbye!

The only thing that can stay in his head longer than a day is a cold.

The only thing you ever made was dandruff.

The only thing you have is "that certain nothing."

The only things you've ever made are cigarette ashes and mistakes.

The only way you'll ever get up in the world is in an airplane.

The reason I eat so much is because I can't stand you on an empty stomach.

The sooner I never see your face again, the better it will be for both of us, when we meet again.

The trouble with you is you're spoiled and you smell the same way.

There is a bus leaving in ten minutes. Try to be under it.

There is a man for you—doesn't smoke, gamble or think.

There are going to be a lot of empty seats at your testimonial dinner.

There is nothing wrong with you that a miracle won't cure.

There is only one thing wrong with your face: it's on the outside.

There is only one thing wrong with you: you're visible.

There is only one way to make me happy: go home!

There was something I liked about you, but you spent it.

There you are. Forgotten but not gone.

Time passes—will you?

Think! It may be a new experience for you.

To succeed you have to get up and go. He never gets up till he has to go.

Too bad you're not lost. I could turn you in for a reward.

Use your head. It's the little things that count!

We are going to miss you around here, but not very much.

We were speaking of monkeys and your name came up.

Well, we all can't be normal.

Well, things could be worse. You could be here in person.

Well, you're in better company than I am.

Were you born by accident, or did your parents really mean it?

What a beautiful dress, dear. Didn't they have it in your size?

What a dummy. He never wrinkles his brow while reading the comics.

What a bore! Your conversation is as dull as a kiss by phone!

What are you doing for a living? You *are* living, aren't you?

What are you eating? It sounds good.

What does your brain want to be when you grow up?

What's new, besides your teeth?

What's on your mind—if you'll forgive the overstatement?

What's the matter? Didn't your dog food agree with you this morning?

What scares me is that sometimes I catch myself enjoying you!

What this country needs is less men like you.

What would you charge to sour a quart of milk?

What you lack in brain you make up in stupidity.

What you need is a personality transplant.

When I look at your face, I wonder what Mother Nature had in mind.

When I want your advice, I'll rattle your cage.

When I want your opinion I'll give it to you.

When you get back home, give my regards to the warden.

When you go home, don't forget to jaywalk.

When you lie down, don't forget to fold your hands.

When you were born, did your doctor know which end to slap?

When you were born something terrible happened. You lived.

Whenever I look at you, I get a terrible desire to be lonesome.

Where did you get that thing on your shoulder? From a used-head dealer?

Where have you been all your life, and why don't you go back there?

Where should I drop you off—on the bridge?

Where were you last seen alive?

Will you please follow the example of your head and come to the point?

With a face like yours, you should send your body to the museum.

With the cost of living so high, why do you bother?

With those ears you look like a taxicab with both doors open.

With those feet you ought to get a job with the government—stamping out forest fires.

With *your* head, you really have it soft.

Who did your nails? Your gardener?

Who gave you this tie? Somebody angry with you?

Who wears your *good* clothes?

Who writes your speeches? An undertaker?

Why be difficult when, with just a little more effort, you can be impossible?

Why do you always wear clothes rejected by the Salvation Army?

Why do you sit here looking like an envelope without any address on it?

Would you mind looking at me? I've got the hiccups.

You always remind me of someone I hate: you!

You are...
     ...a drip and I can't turn you off.
     ...a fine broth of a man; too bad some of the noodles are missing.
     ...a fine dresser, for someone who never buys new clothes.

...a fine guy; I wish I had known you while you were alive.

...a foul ball in the game of life.

...a good egg. There's a lot of yellow in you.

...a man with a mechanical mind. Why didn't you wind it up this morning?

...a mental midget!

...a poor smiling idiot!

...a real treasure and I hope somebody buries you.

...a walking encyclopedia. You can tell us almost nothing about everything.

...about as entertaining as one wrestler.

...about as useless as a pulled tooth.

...as charming as a temporary filling.

...as exciting as a dunked teabag.

...as funny as a bee in a nudist camp.

...as interesting as yesterday's newspaper.

...as loud as a Christmas tie and just as useless.

...as mixed up as scrambled eggs.

...as necessary as a fence around a cemetery.

...as nutty as a whole peanut stand.

...as shallow as a pie pan.

...as silly as a featherweight paperweight.

...as silly as an ostrich courting a sparrow.

...delightfully repulsive.

...dull, unfunny and boring; but in spite of all that, you make me sick.

...foolish to pay what it costs to live.

...harder to ignore than a ringing telephone.

...just what the doctor ordered: shock treatment.

...living proof that man can live without a brain.

...looking fine. Who is your embalmer?

...missing a fine opportunity for keeping quiet.

...nobody's fool, but I'll see if I can get somebody to adopt you.

...not the biggest fool, but you're trying.

...not yourself tonight. I noticed the improvement right away.

...perfect for hot weather. You leave me cold.

...right as rain; in other words, you're all wet.

...so rotten I'm sure you must have invented the toothache.

...so terribly cultured, you can bore me on any subject.

...still dizzy from the ride the stork gave you.

...suffering from poor coordination. Your mouth is too fast for your brain.

...sure a card, why don't you shuffle off?

...the first man I've ever seen with a cauliflower face.

...the kind of a man who would steal the last fan from a fan dancer.

...the kind of person who makes coffee nervous.

...the missing tooth in the smile of happiness.

...the onion on the breath of life.

You can't be two-faced—or you wouldn't be wearing the one you've got!

You could be a perfect understudy for an idiot.

You could be brainwashed with an eyedropper.

You could be the talk of the town if you kill yourself.

You could blow your brain out—you have nothing to lose.

You could make a fortune renting your head out for a balloon.

You could make some lucky girl a happy widow.

You dress beautifully for a man who is obviously colorblind.

You got a good head on your shoulders. You wanna have it chopped off?

You grew up but your brain never did.

You have a charming way of never saying anything intelligent.

You have a clear mind. It isn't cluttered up with facts.

You have a disposition like an untipped waiter.

You have a fine personality, but not for a human being.

You have a fine voice; why spoil it by talking?

You have a great mind; why don't you use it sometimes?

You have a keen sense of stupidity.

You have a lot of funny lines; too bad they're all in your face.

You have a neck like a swan; too bad it isn't as white.

You have a strange growth on your neck, or is it your head?

You have all the possibilities of becoming a complete stranger.

You have as much future as a cake of ice.

You've heard of a "has-been"? He is a "never was."

You have only one bad habit: you breathe!

You still have thirty-two teeth. Would you try for none?

You have that kind of a face, once seen, never remembered.

You have to force yourself not to like him, but it's worth the effort.

You know, even when you're telling the truth, you're lying.

You know, I never thought I would see anything like you without digging.

You know, if you ever lost your face, it would be an improvement!

You know, I've spent a wonderful evening with you the last ten minutes.

You know, they should cover you with chocolate. You're nuts!

You know, they could hold your testimonial dinner in a phone booth.

You know, with the proper amount of coaching you could be a nobody?

You know, you're taking a shortcut to unpopularity?

You know, you're the most complete nothing since the invention of zero?

You know, you could be arrested for impersonating a garbage can?

You know, you could look worse. *I* could have better eyesight.

You know, you've got a fine head on your shoulders. Whose is it?

You know, you sound better when you don't talk.

You know, you would make a perfect stranger!

You look human—unfortunately.

You look like...

> ...a broken handle on the cup of happiness.
> ...a canceled stamp.
> ...a dead-end street.
> ...a detour on the road of life.
> ...a floorwalker in a junk yard.
> ...a freckle on the nose of time.
> ...a human being, but looks can be deceiving.
> ...a jig-saw puzzle that hasn't been put together right.
> ...a loving cup with a big mouth.
> ...a man who got sick during the voyage of his life.
> ...a million. Like a million other jerks.
> ...a permanent toothache.
> ...a Palm Beach suit that's been caught in the rain.
> ...a self-made nobody.
> ...a side dish nobody ordered.
> ...a well-kept grave.
> ...an accident waiting to happen.
> ...an owl and behave like a jackass.
> ...an unmade bed.
> ...the first husband of a widow.
> ...you're walking around just to save funeral expenses.

...you've been under water for six days.
...you fell off a wedding cake.

You look old enough to be your own father.

You look just as bad as your passport photo.

You look sick enough to collect from Blue Cross.

You made a big mistake today. You got out of bed.

You may be a butter and egg man, but you're only a big cheese to me.

You may be a social lion to your friends, but you're just an animal cracker to me.

You may be a tonic to your family, but you're a pill to everyone else.

You must be older than you look; you couldn't get so dumb so fast.

You must have 64 teeth because you have a big mouth.

You must have a big brain to contain so much ignorance.

You needn't wear a hat. Your head is insulated by a vacuum.

You only grew a mustache to break up the monotony of your face.

You only open your mouth when you have nothing to say.

You ought to sleep well, you lie so easily.

You remind me of a splinter. You get under my skin.

You remind me of a toothache I once had.

You remind me of something I want to forget.

You seem to have everything but manners.

You seem to have plenty of get-up and go. So why don't you?

You should be in the movies because you look great in the dark.

You should go to Hollywood. The walk would do you good.

You should really let your hair grow—right over your face.

You sit here like an envelope that doesn't have an address on it.

You sound like water being let out of a tub.

You sound like you've been taking nasty lessons.

You sound like you inherited a million dollars worth of stupidity.

You still look like you did twenty years ago: old!

You sure have a great mind. Too bad it never reached your brain.

You were born with a big handicap: your mouth.

You will never be as old as you look.

You will sure go far; why don't you leave now?

Your brain is on fire; blow it out!

Your clothes don't belong in a closet. They belong in a museum.

Your clothes don't do much for you, but you do even *less* for *them*.

Your face looks better from the back.

Your face looks like you slept in it.

Your face needs a tune-up: your ears are on the wrong way.

Your head is getting too big for your toupee!

Your head looks like a landing field for moths.

Your head looks like you just took it out of the electric mixer.

Your head would look better if you wore it closer to your face.

Your heart is in the right place. It's your head that worries me.

Your ignorance cramps my conversation.

Your parents certainly made a monkey out of you.

Your suit looks like a million, all wrinkled and green.

Your tailor must have had a sense of humor.

Your tongue is sticking out, so why can't you hold it?

Your visit has climaxed an already dull day.

Your voice gives me a pain in the ear.

Insults to a Female

Her voice is too loud for indoor use.

Her voice sounds like a garbage disposal with a spoon caught in it.

She had her ears pierced just for ventilation.

She has a mini-mouth with a maxi-tongue.

She has a personality like...

> ...a brick wall.
> ...a handful of wet sawdust.
> ...a pound of wet liver.
> ...a social disease.
> ...an empty alligator handbag.
> ...an empty shoe box.
> ...the inside of a fountain pen.
> ...warmed-over farina.

She has a voice like a buzz saw striking a rusty nail.

She has shiny hair and a nose to match.

She has that certain far-away look. The further she gets, the better she looks.

She has the same shape as my wallet—flat!

She is a regular clotheshorse. When she puts on her clothes she looks like a horse.

She is as cold as a hot-water bottle in the morning.

She is as cold as a mother-in-law's kiss.

She is as popular as a wet dog in a crowded elevator.

She is as popular as ants on a picnic.

She is as popular as mice at a women's club meeting.

She is as popular as poison ivy in a nudist camp.

She is as sexy as a four-way tablet.

She is as stubborn as a mule.

She is as sweet as a lemon.

She is so skinny, every time she yawns her dress falls off.

She looks like a million, but nobody can be that old!

She must be 40 years old. I counted the rings under her eyes.

She said she is only 35. I wonder if that's her age or her blood pressure.

She should have lived in the dark ages. She looks terrible in the light.

She wears her hair over her shoulder. She should wear it over her face.

She will never have an ulcer. All the acid from her stomach is on her tongue.

The only thing female about her is her name.

Why don't you ...

... act like a man, or don't you do impersonations?

... ask your undertaker for an estimate?

... become a dartlicker for headhunters?

... become a garbage collector and throw yourself into your work?

... blow your nose to ventilate your brain?

... buy a house and stay there?

... buy a jar of vanishing cream and use it?

... buy a one-way ticket to Devil's Island?

... buy some flea powder and commit suicide?

... buy yourself a new broomstick?

... call me over the phone? Let it ring twice and never call again.

... call your keeper to take you back?

... climb the highest mountain and then drop off?

... close the door from the outside?

... close your mouth? I feel a draft.

... close your mouth? You look like a fish.

... comb your hair with a sharp knife?

... come to my New Year's Eve Party? I could use a noisemaker.

... come over for dinner—if you don't mind imposing?

... crawl back into your nightmare?

... crawl back under the rock?

... cross the street blindfolded?

... do me a favor and drop dead?

... do me a favor and stop breathing for a while?

... drink some wet cement?

... drive your car into a brick wall?

... drop dead at your earliest convenience?

... drop down an empty elevator shaft?

... eat apples and bite into worms?

... eat some poison ivy?

... find a nice cliff and jump?

... gargle concrete and let it get hard?

... gargle with old razor blades?

... get a haircut? You look like a chrysanthemum.

... get lost someplace where they have no "found" department?

... get lost in a dense forest?

... get up on the wrong side of an airplane?

... get your brain back from the cleaners?

... get yourself dehydrated?

... give yourself a blood test with an old razor?

... give yourself a hot-foot?

... go and dig a very deep well?

... go around the world on a one-way ticket?

... go away—far, far away?

... go away so far, it would cost me a dollar to send you a postcard?

... go back into the house and stay there?

... go back where you came from—if they'll still take you!

... go downtown and stop revolving doors?

... go home and eat corn on the cob with one hand?

... go home and put your house on fire?

... go home and write yourself some threatening letters?

... go home; your cage must be cleaned by now!

... go jump into the ocean and pull a wave over your head?

... go on a diet and stop eating my heart out?

... go out and bite a mailman?

... go out and get yourself some personality?

... go out and kiss a cactus?

... go out and play with a mad dog?

... go out and slip on the ice pavement?

... go outside and have the doorman take you for a walk?

... go to a photographer and get your negative personality developed?

... go to a window and lean out too far?

... go to a zoo and stay there?

... go to sleep in a waste basket?

... go to a dentist and have some wisdom teeth put in?

... go out and have an accident?

... go out and play in traffic?

... go outside and brush up on your ignorance?

... have a party with all your friends in a phone booth?

... have your suit pressed with you still in it?

... have your tongue pickled?

... have yourself measured for a relapse?

... hit the road and get under a moving car?

... ice skate on very soft ice?

... improve the town by leaving?

... jaywalk on a busy highway?

... just give up living?

... keep your temper? Nobody wants it.

... lay down in front of a steam roller?

... lay down on the track and wait for a train?

... learn to shoot yourself?

... leave and let live?

... lie down for a couple of years?

... light up the whole room by walking out?

... make like a ball and roll away?

... make like a hurricane and blow?

... make me happy by keeping your mouth shut?

... make some lucky girl a happy widow?

... make your wife happy and run away?

... pawn yourself and lose the ticket?

... pick up a drum and beat it?

... play ping-pong with your mouth open?

... play your electric guitar in the bathtub?

... put your hair on a stick and mop the floor with it?

... pull yourself together, or isn't it worth the trouble?

... put a rope around your neck and tighten it?

... put a rubber band around your neck and snap out of it?

... put your best foot forward so I can step on it?

... put your brain into a freezer?

... put your glasses on backwards and walk into yourself?

... put your head between your hands and applaud?

... put your teeth in backwards and bite yourself?

... read a blank book and improve your mind?

... rent yourself out to haunt a house?

... resign from the human race?

... say goodbye?

... send your wits out to be sharpened?

... settle down in a garbage can?

··· shrink your head and use it as a paperweight?

··· start out on a road to nowhere?

··· sit down and rest your best talent?

· sit down and take a mess off your feet?

··· sit on a metal chair and plug it in?

··· step outside for a few years?

··· step in front of a moving steam roller and iron your brain?

··· stick some dynamite into your ears and blow your brain apart?

··· stick your head out the window—feet first?

··· smell an exhaust pipe for hours?

··· smoke some gun powder and blow your brain out?

··· sneeze? Your brain is rusty.

··· sue your brain for nonsupport?

··· take a bath in a cement mixer?

··· take a bath in quicksand?

··· take a big step out the window?

··· take a long walk on a short pier?

··· take a nap on a railroad track?

··· take a nap under a falling axe?

··· take a powder—like arsenic?

··· take a taxi home and don't tip the driver?

··· take a vacation, say for about ten years?

··· take the elevator and stop between floors?

··· take the elevator downstairs and stay there?

··· take the next broom out of town?

··· take three giant steps out the window?

··· throw your hat away and keep your head in it?

··· tie your shoelaces in a revolving door?

... touch a live wire with wet hands?

... trade in your head for a bowling ball?

... turn around and go straight home?

... turn the other way; I have a weak stomach.

... use the nearest fire exit?

... visit a near-sighted knife thrower?

... wait for a speeding car while crossing the street?

... walk around the block until a car hits you?

... walk across the Hudson River?

... walk into a closed door?

... walk into a parking meter and violate yourself?

... walk over an open manhole?

... walk until your hat floats?

... wear your socks to bed to keep your brain warm?

Stinging Curses

May a rash cover your entire body as you leave your house today.

May all your baths be too hot and all your women too cold.

May all your relatives move in with you.

May all your shoes be too long and your haircuts too short.

May you be a liar with a poor memory.

May you be the proof that man can endure everything.

May you bargain with God and lose.

May you become famous—in medical history.

May you become like a lamp, to hang all day and burn all night.

May everything you cook stick to the bottom of the pan.

May student barbers practice on your beard.

May the bird of happiness fly in your mouth and lay an egg there.

May the bird of paradise fly up your nose.

May the day you were born be erased from the calendar.

May you break a leg and lose your crutch.

May you grow like an onion, with your head in the ground and your feet in the air.

May you have to spend many hours in a soft chair—at your dentist.

May you jump with joy—and right into an open manhole.

May you lose all your teeth except one—the one with the toothache.

May you take a nice walk and stumble on a skunk.

May you turn into a centipede with ingrown toenails.

May you always dream of troubles when you sleep.

May you always bite into the worms while eating apples.

May your appetite enlarge and your digestion diminish.

May your hat be the right size, but your head too small.

May your sex life be as good as your credit.

May your wife be as much help to you as a lame horse.

May your wife eat toast in bed and may you roll in crumbs.

He is so cheap . . .

. . .   after shaking your hand he counts his fingers.

. . .   before counting his money he gets drunk so he'll see double.

. . .   after he walked six miles to the ballpark, he was too tired to jump over the fence.

. . .   even his 8 by 10 photos are only 7 by 9.

. . .   even if he was in a canoe he wouldn't tip.

. . .   for an icepack he only uses one cube.

. . .   for supper he sits out on the porch and bites his lips.

. . .   he always counts his money in front of a mirror so he won't cheat himself.

. . .   he always licks his eye glasses after eating grapefruit.

... he always swallows his food without chewing to save wear and tear on his teeth.

... he always takes long steps to save on shoe leather.

... he always washes his paper plates.

... he always wears mittens so money won't slip through his fingers.

... he bought a watermelon, put some feathers on it and told his kids it was a turkey.

... he bought his daughter a doll house with a mortgage on it.

... he called up his girl friend to find out which night she was free......

... he decided to become a divorce lawyer so he could get a free woman.

... he drycleans Kleenex.

... he even saves broken shoelaces.

... he even stops his watch to save time.

... he fed his cat salted peanuts so it would drink water instead of milk.

... he gave his children violin lessons so they won't have to get haircuts.

... he gave his horse green glasses and then fed him straw to make him believe it was grass.

... he goes to a costume ball as Napoleon so he can keep his hand on his wallet.

... he goes to a drugstore and buys one Kleenex.

... he got married in his own backyard so his chicken could get the rice.

... he has a burglar alarm system on his garbage can.

... he has a coin slot on his bathroom door for visitors.

... he has a slight impediment in his reach.

... he heats his knives so he won't use too much butter.

... he is a man of rare gifts. It's rare when he gives one.

... he is tighter than the top olive in the bottle.

... he is waiting for the Encyclopedia Britannica to come out in paperback.

... he is waiting for a total eclipse of the sun so he can send a night-rate telegram.

... he keeps a moth as a pet because it only eats holes.

... he keeps his finger nails extra short so he has a hard time picking up a check.

... he keeps his piggy bank in the safe.

... he learned the Braille system so he can read in the dark.

... he left his home town as a barefoot boy and came back ten years later for his shoes.

... he married a girl born February 29, so he only has to buy her a birthday present every four years.

... he married a skinny girl so he could get a small wedding ring.

... he married his secretary so he wouldn't have to give her a Christmas bonus.

... he never eats asparagus in a restaurant so he won't have to leave tips.

... he never enjoys dessert in a restaurant; it's too close to the check.

... he never wears suspenders or a belt, so he has to keep his hands in his pockets.

... he only goes to a drive-in movie in the daytime.

... he only rides the subway during rush hours to get his clothes pressed.

... he only takes outdoor photographs when it's lightning.

... he only wears clothes with one-way pockets.

... he opened his pocketbook and three moths flew out.

... he puts boric acid in his grapefruit to get a free eye wash.

... he puts glue in his mustache so his kisses will last longer.

... he quit golf when he lost his ball.

... he reaches for a check like it was a subpoena.

... he remarried his wife so he wouldn't have to pay any more alimony.

... he rethreads his old shoelaces.

... he saved all his toys for his second childhood.

... he says his prayers once a year and the rest of the year he only says, "Ditto."

... he shakes hands with only one finger.

... he shot his parents so he could go to an orphan's picnic.

... he shows his children a picture of a cake on their birthdays.

... he spends hours before his TV set, but he never turns it on.

... he takes his date out to see a fire.

... he takes his electric razor to the office to recharge it.

... he takes his girl to a drive-in restaurant and then won't open the windows.

... he talks through his nose to save wear and tear on his teeth.

... he tears off the month of December on his calendar to fool his children.

... he thinks he's treating when he pays his own check.

... he took his children out of school because they had to pay attention.

... he took his girl to a hardware store to pick out a ring.

... he took his girl for a taxi ride and she was so beautiful, he could hardly keep his eyes on the meter.

... he took his girl to a movie and got so excited that he almost paid for his ticket.

... he took out some fire insurance on his cigars.

... he tried to get a 13¢ stamp wholesale.

... he uses the same calendar year after year.

... he waits for an eclipse to develop his film.

... he waits for lightning to read his paper at night.

... he walks his date to a drive-in movie.

... he holds an umbrella over his sheep when it was raining so the wool won't shrink.

... he wears a vest to keep his money as close as possible to his heart.

... he went alone on his honeymoon.

... he will always sit with his back to the check.

... he will never finish his soup, so that he won't have to tip the plate.

... he will never lend a hand.

... he won't even give his wife an argument.

... he won't even let you borrow trouble.

... he won't even pay attention.

... he won't even tip his hat.

... he won't laugh unless it's at somebody else's expense.

... he would come over and borrow a flag on July 4th.

... he would give a nudist a pocket watch.

... he would have asked for separate checks at the Last Supper.

... he would never even pass the buck.

... he would stick his head into an electric mixer to save the price of a haircut.

... he wouldn't even spend Christmas.

... he wouldn't give a duck a drink even if he owned Lake Michigan.

... he wouldn't send his pajamas to the laundry unless he had a pair of socks stuck in the pocket.

... he wouldn't take a drink out of a bottle because it has to be tipped.

... his money doesn't go to his head because it never leaves his pocket.

... in fact, he is tighter than a train window.

... the only thing he ever gave away was a secret.

... the only thing he ever paid was a compliment.

... the only thing he ever spends on a girl is passion.

... the only thing he ever threw out was the bill collector.

... the only thing he ever took out was his teeth.

... the only things he puts on the table when company comes are ashtrays.

... the only time he buys a round of drinks is when he's alone.

... the only time he puts his own hands in his pockets is during cold days.

... the only time he will pick up the check is when it is made out to him.

... they call him the "dollar a year" man—because that's all he ever spends.

... they were married 35 years and the last present he gave his wife was a wedding ring.

... to save feeding them, he sent his flock of homing pigeons out and then moved.

... to save money on the laundry bill, he puts soap flakes in all his pockets and walked through a car wash once a week.

...   when he feels sick he goes to stores and reads get-well cards.

...   when he found a box of corn plasters, he went out and bought a pair of tight shoes.

...   when he pays you a compliment he asks for a receipt.

...   when he says he's eating out it means eating on the fire escape.

...   when he sends Christmas Cards they read, "A Merry Christmas for all the coming years!"

4

Wisecracks

Food

A fly in the soup is better than no meat at all.

A hardboiled egg is hard to beat.

A short waiter makes the steaks look bigger.

An onion a day gives your diet away.

Eating used to be a necessity, then it became a luxury and now it's an investment.

Everything comes to him who orders hash.

Food nowadays is so expensive, it's cheaper to eat money.

It is sure bad manners to dip bread in the gravy, but it's such good taste.

It's better to have hair in your soup than soup in your hair.

Mustard is no good without roast beef.

No formal dinner is complete without nuts—invite a few.

No matter how you slice it, a pizza is too hot to eat when you start and too cold when you finish.

Soup should be seen and not heard.

The best thing to put in a homemade pie is your teeth.

The only thing that looks good in a brown jacket is a potato.

They say if you eat vegetables for 80 years you won't die young.

To eat is human; to digest, divine.

Too many cooks spoil the figure.

When you've eaten onions, don't wear a rose in your buttonhole.

General

A barking dog never bites—while barking.

A bathing beauty is a girl worth wading for.

A bathing beauty points out the figures, but slacks reveal the facts.

A bird in hand is bad table manners.

A bird in hand is worthless when you want to blow your nose.

A bird in hand lays no eggs, but two in the bush build a nest.

A black eye is a stamp of disapproval.

A blotter is something you look for while the ink dries.

A clever man can throw his weight around without losing his balance.

A clever man tells a woman he understands her; a stupid man tries to prove it.

A confidential secretary is one your wife never finds out about.

A corn on the ear is worth two on the toe.

A drink in the hand is worth two bucks in the night club.

A fine is a tax for doing wrong; a tax is a fine for doing well.

A first kiss is something that comes only once in a lifetime.

A friend in need is a friend to keep away from.

A friend in need is a pest indeed.

A friend is a friend until he borrows money.

A gas station used to clean our windshield instead of our wallet.

A good listener is the best talker.

A hair in the head is worth two in the brush.

A hanky in your hand is worth two in the drawer.

A kiss is the shortest distance between two.

A kiss that speaks volumes is seldom a first edition.

A powdered nose is no guarantee of a clean neck.

A rolling stone gathers no boss.

A rolling stone makes strange bedfellows.

A stitch in time is a girl's best friend.

A stitch in time makes bending safer.

A stitch in time saves embarrassing exposure.

A thing of beauty is a great expense.

A troublemaker never has any trouble making trouble.

Absent friends makes the liquor last longer.

After a gambler has lost his shirt, he can't expect to eat on the cuff.

After the boat reaches the middle of the river, it's too late to fix the leak.

Alimony will do you no good on a cold night.

Always getting into hot water will cook your goose.

An ounce of keep-your-mouth-shut beats a ton of explanation.

An unwelcome guest is one of the best things going.

Anybody who wakes up and finds himself famous hasn't been asleep.

As ye sew, so shall ye rip.

As you slide down the banister of life, may the splinter never point the wrong way.

Be thankful you are not a centipede with fallen arches.

Be thankful you are not a giraffe with a sore throat.

Be thankful you are not an elephant with sinus trouble.

Be true to your teeth, or they'll be false to you.

Beauty isn't everything, but it is sure nice to look at.

Before marriage a girl has to kiss her man to hold him; after marriage she has to hold him to kiss him.

Before you knock on wood see if the doorbell works.

Ben Franklin discovered electricity, but the person that invented the meter made all the money.

Better be silent and be thought a fool than to speak and remove all doubt.

Big noses usually run in some families.

Bowling is the second most popular indoor sport.

Bread cast upon the water clogs up the pipes.

Brush your hair after every meal and see your barber twice a year.

Cold baths are more enjoyable when taken with hot water.

Despite all complaints about the high cost of living, most people still think it's worth it.

Dieting means to starve to death in order to live a little longer.

Doctors claim drinking is bad for us, but I have seen more old drunks around than old doctors.

Doing a comedy routine without an audience is like playing handball without a wall.

Don't forget that the peacock of today is the feather duster of tomorrow.

Even when opportunity knocks, you still have to get up to open the door.

Everybody knows everything better than anybody.

Everyone wants to go to Heaven, but no one wants to die.

Everything is nervous nowadays. Even my watch has a tick.

Except when I'm wrong, I'm always right.

Footprints on the sand of time are not made sitting down.

For a mother the son always shines.

Gardeners with green thumbs often have black and blue knees.

Good, clear handwriting is a handicap if you can't spell.

Great aches from little toe corns grow.

Growing old isn't so bad when you consider the alternative.

Half a loaf is better than no vacation at all.

Halitosis is better than no breath at all.

He is a big ear doctor, looks only at big ears.

Hitting the ceiling is no way to get up in the world.

I always find lost things in the last place I look, so I'm looking there first.

I always drive with the emergency brakes on. When an emergency happens, I'm ready.

I always wear sunglasses on rainy days. It protects my eyes from umbrellas.

I can lift an elephant with one hand, but I can't find an elephant with one hand.

I don't understand it: at gas stations they keep the register wide open but the men's room is locked.

I may look busy, but I'm only confused.

I never get lost—everyone tells me where to go!

I was trying to get a new car for my wife but nobody would swap.

I'm getting so accustomed to being tense that when I'm calm I get nervous.

In Hollywood there are three groups of people: the Have-beens, the Are-nows, and the May-be's.

In two days tomorrow will be yesterday.

It is better to let things go as they depart then to take them as they come.

It is hard keeping your shirt on trying to get something off your chest.

It is proven that 100 percent of the chain smokers prefer cigarettes to chains.

It's time to face the music when a note is due.

It isn't the *cost* of a strapless gown—it's the upkeep.

It was an ideal divorce: she got the children and he got the maid.

It's always the last key that opens the lock.

It's an ill wind that blows the minute you leave the hairdresser.

It's better to be over the hill than under it.

It's better to have something to remember than nothing to forget.

It's better to tighten your belt than to lose your pants.

It's funny, we never get too old to learn new ways to be stupid.

It's much better to have your hands on a gal than a gal on your hand.

It's remarkable that cold feet are often the result of burned fingers.

I've had bad luck with both my wives. The first divorced me and the second won't.

Keeping your chin up prevents gravy from dripping on your clothes.

Labor Day is a day when nobody does any.

Late hours are bad for one but nice for two.

Laughter is an inexpensive way to improve your health.

Learning to play the harp is no guarantee that you'll go to heaven.

Let a smile be your umbrella if you like to gargle snow.

Let him among us who runs the fastest throw the first stone.

Love is a three-ring circus: engagement ring, wedding ring and suffering.

Love is an itch around the heart that can't be scratched.

Love is awful to be in but even worse to be out of.

Love is blind and marriage is an eye opener.

Love is like a mushroom: you're never sure whether it's the real thing until it's too late.

Love is like an ocean of emotion entirely surrounded by expenses.

Love makes a man spoon, but it's matrimony which makes him fork over.

Love may make the world go round, but so does a punch in the nose.

Many a thing of beauty becomes a jaw forever.

Many a true word is spoken through false teeth.

Many are called but only after the horse is stolen.

Many are called for but few get the right number.

Many are cold but few are frozen.

Marriage agrees with me, but my wife never does.

Marriage brings music in a man's life. He learns how to play second fiddle.

Marriage is a great institution; no family should be without it.

Marriage is a union of two people. So how come the man has to pay all the dues?

Marriage is just like a car: it starts with a license and ends with a wreck.

Marriage is like a violin. After the beautiful music is over, the strings are still attached.

Marriage is like a warm bath. Once you get used to it, it's not so hot.

Marriage is no gamble. When you're gambling you can win once in awhile.

Marriage is popular because it combines the maximum of temptation with the maximum of opportunities.

Marriage is a real grind. You wash dishes, make the beds and two weeks later you have to do it all over again.

Marriage is the most expensive way to get your laundry free.

Marriages are happy. It's the living together afterwards that causes all the trouble.

Married life is great! It's my wife I can't stand!

May all your troubles last as long as your New Year's resolutions.

May you have a holiday you'll always remember and a hangover you'll never forget.

My best friend married my sister; now he hates me like a brother.

My boss gave me a pink slip but what I really needed was a sweatshirt.

My father always listens to my mother. He has to. She never stops talking.

My mind is made up. Don't confuse me with the facts!

My wife doesn't care for money. As soon as I give it to her, she goes out and spends it.

Nice guys finish last. So do people who read instructions.

No customer can be worse than no customer.

No horse can go as fast as the money you bet on him.

No matter how far you travel you only move two feet.

No matter how hot the day is, at night it gets dark.

No matter what kind of coal you use, it always goes up in smoke.

Nobody has ever complained about a parachute not opening.

Nothing can hold liquor as well as the bottle.

Nothing cooks your goose quicker than a boiling temper.

Nothing is as useless as a pulled tooth.

Nothing lasts as long as a necktie you don't like.

Now they have a jig-saw puzzle for people you don't like. None of the pieces fit and the four corners are missing.

Nowadays a thoughtful bride saves a piece of her wedding cake for her divorce lawyer.

Of the many ways to treat a cold, advice is the least effective.

One good turn gets the whole blanket.

One half of something is better than all of nothing.

One thing about Columbus: he didn't miss the boat.

One thing you can still get for a dime is two nickels.

One way to keep happy is to learn to enjoy trouble.

One way to lose your shirt is to put too much on the cuff.

Only a friend can become an enemy—a relative is one from the beginning.

Opportunities knock once and the neighbors the rest of the time.

Ostrich that keeps head in sand too long gets burned in end.

Our refrigerator makes so many cubes, I can't believe my own ice.

Oversleeping will never make your dreams come true.

Poor handwriting covers up a lot of mistakes in spelling.

Push will get a person everywhere except through a door marked *Pull.*

Remember, you have to be wise before you can be witty!

She couldn't afford a divorce so she shot him.

Some golfers use carts instead of caddies because carts can't count.

Some men need two women in their life: a secretary to take things down, and a wife to pick things up.

Sometimes it is better to have loved and lost than to have to do homework for three children.

Success is relative. The more success, the more relatives.

Sunshine and moonshine makes your nose red.

The best time to buy a used car is when it's new.

The best time to miss a train is at a crossing.

The big guns of business are usually those who have never been fired.

The chief cause of all divorces is matrimony.

The female of the speeches is more deadly than the male.

The home circle can never be kept square with a triangle.

The housing shortage is just a rumor started by people who have no place to live.

The hurrier you go, the behinder you get.

The liquor of today is the hangover of tomorrow.

The most dangerous way to cross the street is on foot.

The only thing worse than a flooded basement is a flooded attic.

The penalty for bigamy is having two mothers-in-law.

The road to success is always under construction.

The worst things about television are the sponsors who make the impossible programs possible.

There are millions of reasons why women dress the way they do, and all of them are men.

There are two things my wife wore once and then put away forever: her wedding dress and her apron.

There is a stairway to success but everybody is looking for the elevator.

There's a big difference between going to pieces and falling apart!

There's only one thing that's easy to get these days and that's confused.

There's only one trouble with the United Nations—too many foreigners in it.

They remarried. We *knew* the divorce wouldn't last.

Those who complain about the way the ball bounces are usually the ones who dropped it.

Those who say "You can't take it with you," don't know how to pack a car for a vacation trip.

Those who sleep in the raw are in for a nude awakening.

To itch is human, to scratch divine.

To keep lipstick from smearing, eat a lot of garlic.

To keep your cat litter smelling fresh—get rid of the cat!

To leave footsteps in the sand of time you have to be on your toes.

To make your hat look smaller wear a bigger head.

To make your shoes look smaller get smaller feet.

To prevent a cold in the head from going into your chest just tie a knot in your neck.

Traffic tickets are like wives. Nobody complains about them until he gets one of his own.

We really don't need any calendars. When it rains, it's Sunday.

We seldom feather our nest by going on a wild goose chase.

When Congress makes a joke it's a law. And when they make a law it's a joke.

When everybody is somebody then nobody is anybody.

When it comes to cars, many people start something they can't stop.

When it comes to work, there are many who will stop at nothing.

When out driving watch the curves. Don't feel them.

When someone kicks you from behind it proves you're out in front.

When you carry a glass bottle don't sit on a stone bench.

When you get something for nothing, you just haven't been billed for it yet.

When you intend to blow your top, don't wear a toupee.

When you roll up your sleeves you seldom lose your shirt.

Whenever a bartender makes a mistake a new drink is born.

Whiskey may not cure a cold, but no remedy fails with such satisfaction.

Whiskey may shorten your life, but you'll see twice as much in half the time.

Women's clothing has been compared to a barbed-wire fence. It serves its purpose without obstructing any of the view.

Work is the crabgrass in the lawn of life.

You can save yourself a lot of trouble by not borrowing any.

You can't drive a nail with a sponge, no matter how long you soak it!

You can't fall out of bed if you sleep on the floor.

You can't make a hit if you have no aim in life.

You can't save your face if you lose your head.

You should always be sincere whether you mean it or not.

You will never hit the mark if you don't pull the trigger.

You will never stub your toe walking backwards.

Your ship won't come in until you row out to meet it.

Youth is a wonderful thing. It is a crime to waste it on children.

Girls

A girl can either go to the mountain and see the scenery or go to the beach and be the scenery.

A girl cannot get married without dragging some poor fellow down the aisle.

A girl in a car is worth more than five in the phone book.

A girl in good shape is the reason for many men being in bad shape.

A girl in your lap is worth two in your mind.

A girl is getting old when she begins to worry more about how her shoes fit than how her sweater fits.

A girl nowadays has to keep on her toes to avoid heels.

A girl should wait for the right man, but should get married meanwhile if she can.

A girl wants a man who is smart enough to make a lot of money and stupid enough to give it to her.

A girl who is a picture of health usually has a nice frame.

A girl who is expecting a ring will always answer the phone.

A girl who knows all the answers is often asked something out of the question.

A girl who plays with fire seldom strikes a match.

A girl who thinks no man is good enough for her may be right, but she is more often left.

A girl with cold feet does a lot of walking.

A girl's face may be her fortune but the other parts draw interest.

A good girl is good but a bad girl is better.

A green girl in pink condition can give a fellow the blues.

A miss in the car is worth two in the engine.

A modern girl in a modern dress puts more and more in less and less.

Anatomy is something that everybody has, but it looks better on a girl.

Any girl who knows how to cook can find a man who knows how to eat.

Girls' fashions may change but their design remains the same.

Girls make better wives than anybody.

Girls who have already tried everything under the sun to land a husband should try it under the moon.

Girls who say, "Nothing doing!" are the ones who spends evenings doing nothing.

Girls who try to be talking encyclopedias should remember that reference books are never taken out.

Girls with figures make the best dates.

Many a bathing girl has gotten into deep water.

Many a blonde dyes by her own hand.

Many a girl goes out on a moonlight date and comes home in a fog.

Many a girl has gotten first-hand information in a second-hand car.

Many a girl is more than tickled when her boy friend calls.

Many a girl, these days, goes into an office looking for a position and finds herself in a situation.

Many a girl thinks she is sitting pretty when her knees show.

Many a girl who doesn't get taken out has an appendix that does.

Many a girl should stop looking for an ideal husband and should start looking for a single man.

Nothing makes a girl watch her figure more than men who don't.

Now the only sweater girls who'll date me knit them—not wear them.

Some girls are easy to look at, while others pull down their shades.

Some girls are famous for their beautiful ayes!

Some girls are hard to please. If you don't give them the world, they give you the gate.

Some girls are like boxers. They won't go into action until they see a ring.

Some girls are like flowers—they grow wild in the woods.

Some girls are like paint. Get them all stirred up and you can't get them off your hands.

Some girls are like typewriters. Press the wrong place and you get terrible words.

Some girls are looking for a husband with a fat wallet and a slim stomach.

Some girls are not afraid of mice; others have pretty legs.

Some girls are sure hard to figure out, but it's sure interesting research.

Some girls are very broad-minded when it comes to a narrow sofa.

Some girls blush when they shouldn't, but most girls don't blush when they should.

Some girls can be had for a song: the "Wedding March."

Some girls count on their fingers and others count on their legs.

Some girls get a man into a jam and then let him down with a jar.

Some girls have hour-glass figures, while others look like alarm clocks.

Some girls have such good figures they get the once-over twice.

Some girls have what it takes, to take what you have.

Some girls know little about making bread but more about needing dough.

Some girls may not know how to cook, but they'll know what's cooking.

Some girls of today are not what they were ten years ago. Some are two years older.

Some girls play hard to get until they become hard to take.

Some girls today wear less on the street than their grandmothers did in bed.

Some girls who are the picture of health are just painted that way.

Some girls who can't swim a stroke will know every dive in town.

Some girls will play post office only if the male is First Class.

Some girls will turn a man's head with their charm and his stomach with their cooking.

Some girls use a lot of soap to get a ring around their fingers.

Some girls wait so long for their ships to come in, that their piers collapse.

Take your choice: be an old maid and look for a husband every day, or marry and look for him every night.

The girl who lacks the nerve to wear a strapless gown usually lacks the figure too.

The girl with a future avoids a man with a past.

The old-fashioned girl darned her husband's socks. The modern girl socks her darned husband.

To most girls, men are not a problem but a solution.

Today a girl has a hard time trying to look as young as her mother.

Usually the girl who "no's" knows.

What every girl should know is better.

When a girl begins to count on a man, his number is up.

When a girl calls you by your first name, she is out for your last.

Husbands

A husband is sometimes just as hard to find after marriage as before.

A husband is what is left over from a sweetheart after the nerve has been removed.

A husband should tell his wife everything that he is sure she will find out, before anyone else does.

A husband who boasts that he runs things around the house is probably talking about the lawnmower.

A husband who gets breakfast in bed is in the hospital.

A husband who is busy as a bee may wake up and find his honey missing.

A husband who puts his foot down probably had it on the coffee table.

A husband would rather come home and find the refrigerator on the blink than come home and find the iceman out of order.

A rich husband is always a rich man but a rich man is often a poor husband.

A smart husband hides his money in clothes that need mending.

A wise husband buys his wife such expensive China, she won't trust him to wash the dishes.

Many a poor husband was once a rich bachelor.

Many a husband would be satisfied if he had the income his wife hopes the neighbors think he has.

More husbands would leave home if they knew how to pack suitcases.

The average husband is one who lays down the law to his wife and then accepts all her amendments.

The husband who talks in his sleep may just be taking advantage of his opportunity.

You cannot make a husband tender by keeping him in hot water.

Life

It is better to live rich than to die rich.

It is better to make mistakes than not to live at all.

Life is a big struggle to support a wife and the government at the same time.

Life is a continuous process of getting used to things we hadn't expected.

Life is a dream; wake up!

Life is a pickle; preserve it!

Life is a sentence that man must serve for the crime of being born.

Life is a stage; don't get stagefright!

Life is a time period in which the first half is ruined by our parents and the second half by our children.

Life is an everlasting struggle to keep money coming in and teeth and hair from falling out.

Life is full of ups and downs—like getting up in the morning and getting down to work.

Life is like a game of golf. As soon as you get out of one hole you start heading for another.

Life is like a shower. One wrong turn and you're in hot water.

Life is like a taxi. The meter keeps going whether you're getting somewhere or just standing still.

Life is really wonderful; don't miss it if you can.

Life is so uncertain these days that the only thing you can really count on for sure are your fingers.

Life is very colorful. The traffic lights are red and green, and the pedestrians are black and blue.

Life is what passes you by while you're making other plans.

Life is wonderful. Without it you'd be dead.

Living a double life will get you nowhere twice as fast.

When life hands you a lemon, make lemonade.

When my old flame walked into my married life we had a big explosion.

You should live like a fried egg—with your sunny side up.

Man

A man calls himself a bachelor until he gets married. *Then* you should hear what he calls himself!

A man can always tell what kind of time he has at a party by the look on his wife's face.

A man can drop a lot of money trying to pick up a little honey.

A man goes through three stages: he believes in Santa, he doesn't believe in Santa, he is Santa!

A man in love is bound to be bound.

A man in love is no judge of beauty.

A man is a person who falls in love with a beautiful face and makes the mistake of marrying the whole girl.

A man is as old as he feels before breakfast. A woman is as old as she looks before breakfast.

A man is incomplete until he's married—then he's really finished.

A man is just like a candle: he smokes too much, not bright when lit, and always goes out when needed most.

A man is known by the company he is trying to avoid.

A man is known by the company he thinks nobody knows he's keeping.

A man is known by the company his wife keeps.

A man never knows what he can do until he tries to undo what he's done.

A man should work eight hours a day and sleep eight a day—but not the same eight hours.

A man who brags he never made a mistake has a wife who did.

A man who can drive safely while kissing a pretty girl isn't giving the kiss the attention it deserves.

A man who falls in love with himself has no mother-in-law.

A man who gives in when he's right is married.

A man who had not kissed his wife in years shot a man who did.

A man who is buried in thoughts generally has a grave appearance.

A man who knows everything under the sun usually has shadows under his eyes.

A man who laughs last doesn't get the joke.

A man who laughs last usually has a tooth missing.

A man who loves rich food and cooks it, looks it.

A man who marries a chicken gets henpecked.

A man who marries for money earns it.

A man who marries to have someone to tell his troubles to, soon has plenty to talk about.

A man who misses his mother-in-law doesn't throw straight.

A man who never makes a mistake can't be very busy.

A man who puts his nose to the grindstone is a bloody fool.

A man who says talk is cheap never hired a lawyer.

A man who sits on a hot stove will rise again.

A man who steals my purse steals cash.

A man who thinks by inch and talks by yard deserves to be kicked by foot.

A man who thinks marriage is a 50:50 proposition doesn't know the half of it.

A man with holes in his socks is usually married to a woman who doesn't give a darn.

A man's body is extremely sensitive. Pat him on the back and his head swells.

A man's problem while his wife is making a splash is to keep his head above water.

A married man is one who uses both hands to drive his car.

A real gourmet is a man who puts salt and pepper on his toothpaste.

A wise man never blows his knows.

A wise man never laughs at his wife's old clothes.

All men are not homeless, but some are home less than others.

Any man who claims he knows all the answers hasn't heard all the questions.

Any man who marries again doesn't deserve to lose his first wife.

Behind every successful man stands a surprised wife.

Behind every successful man stands a wife with a handful of bills.

Being rich is no good. A man with one watch knows what time it is. A man with two watches is never sure.

By the time a man is rich enough to sleep late, he's too old to enjoy it.

Even if a man could understand women, he still wouldn't believe it.

Every man should have a wife, preferably his own.

Man is the only animal that can be skinned more than once.

Many a man believes in dreams until he marries one.

Many a man drinks only to forget the woman who is driving him to drink.

Many a man goes into a bar for an eye-opener and comes out blind.

Many a man has acquired a huge vocabulary by marrying.

Many a man has burned his fingers trying to grab the Toast of the Town.

Many a man knows *how* to kiss a girl, but not *when*.

Many a man loses his balance when his wife goes shopping.

Many a man tries to escape the sea of matrimony by drinking like a fish.

Many a man who has asked for a girl's hand finds himself under her thumb.

Many a man who kicked about having to mow the lawn all summer will soon be bellowing about having to fire the furnace.

Many a man who opened a conversation with a girl years ago is now wondering how he can shut her off.

Many a man suspects his wife married him to give her mother a home.

Married men make the best husbands.

Most men regard blondes as golden opportunities.

No man lives long enough to do all the things his wife wants him to do.

No matter how busy a man is, he's never too busy to stop and talk about how busy he is.

Not all men are fools. Some are bachelors.

Nothing is impossible to the man who doesn't have to do it.

Nothing upsets a man's balance as much as a wife who likes to write checks.

One man's junk is another man's rare antique.

One man's telephone is another man's wrong number.

Some men are summer workers. Summer working and summer not.

Some men can't think straight. They always have curves on their mind.

Some men get what they deserve—others remain single.

Some men like to go fishing while others do their drinking at home.

The average man marries his girl because he can't afford to take her out any longer.

The bigger a man's head gets, the easier it is to fill his shoes.

The clothes that make a woman break a man.

The first thing a man makes in his workshop is a mess.

The happiest marriage would be the union of a deaf man and a blind woman.

The man who can swallow an aspirin at a drinking fountain deserves to get well.

The man who would rather play golf than eat should marry a woman who would rather play bridge than cook.

The man with the smallest idea and the biggest mouth gets the most attention.

This is still a free country where a man can do as his wife pleases.

When a man brings flowers to his wife for no reason, there's a reason.

When a man drinks, he does it for two reasons: either he has no wife or he has.

When a man needs a friend he often makes a mistake and gets a wife.

When a man pats you on the back, he's figuring out where to stick the knife.

When a man says his business is run down it means he's going to wind it up.

When a man stays late at the office, he is either trying to finish something or trying to start something.

Money

A dime is valuable today, especially if you want to put in your two cents worth.

A dollar goes very fast nowadays, but not very far.

A penny saved gathers no moss.

Anybody who can afford to pay interest these days doesn't need a loan.

By the time you have found the key to success, someone has changed the lock.

By the time you have money to burn, the fire has gone out.

Credit is a clever financial trick that enables us to spend what we haven't got.

Enjoy today to the fullest. They may cancel your credit card tomorrow.

It doesn't matter if you are born poor and die poor, as long as you are rich in between.

It is easy to save pennies today. What else can you do with them?

It's easy to make money. It's hard to make a living.

Kissing may be the language of love, but money still does the talking.

Mom's spending capacity is greater than Dad's earning capacity.

Money can't buy happiness, but have you tried to buy anything without it?

Money doesn't care who has it.

Money is green stuff with pictures of dead people on it.

Money is like fertilizer; it's no good unless you spread it around.

Money is not for poor people.

Money is something that only millionaires don't need.

Money is worth so little now that it's surprising that so many people spend so much time working for it.

Money isn't everything. Henry Ford with all his money never owned a Cadillac.

Money isn't important as long as you have it.

Money means nothing to me. Every time my wife asks for money, she gets nothing.

Money sure talks. But to me it only says goodbye!

My boss cheated me out of a fortune. He wouldn't let me marry his daughter.

My paycheck is like tide—it comes in and goes out.

Our floating currency is a sign of sinking economy.

Silence is golden but money talks.

The hardest thing to get hold of these days is easy money.

The less you bet, the more you lose when you win.

The only thing you can do without money is get into debt.

The other fellow's wallet always looks greener.

The outcome of the income depends on the outgo for the upkeep.

There is still one thing you can get for a dime: An eight-cent stamp.

There's no place like home—if you haven't got the money to go out.

When your outgo exceeds your income then your upkeep is your downfall.

Whether rich or poor, it's nice to have money.

People

It is easy to see through people who make spectacles of themselves.

Many people are so restless, they don't feel at home at home.

Many people get gray worrying over gray hair.

Many people have social circles under their eyes.

No one is as busy as the person who has nothing to do.

People are more fun than anybody.

People who go away to study singing should.

People like to hear the truth no matter how flattering it is.

People who live in stone houses shouldn't throw glasses.

People who say they are going on a diet are just wishful shrinkers.

People who throw kisses are lazy.

People would be in better health if they didn't get sick so much.

The more we think of people, the less we think of them.

The only person who beats time is a drum player.

The only thing that comes to people who sit and wait is gray hair.

The world is divided into two kinds of people. Those in the swim and those in the soup.

They say people who have the most money are the richest people in the world.

When four people get together, a fifth is usually welcome.

Wives

A wife can make a home more attractive by hiring a pretty maid.

A wife laughs at her husband's jokes not because they are clever, but because *she* is.

A wife sees red whenever she finds a blonde hair on her husband's coat.

Anybody can kiss his own wife but the iceman has his pick.

Arguing with a wife is like trying to blow out a light bulb.

Be kind to your wife; she may help you with the dishes.

Giving my wife a credit card is like giving a cat its own fish market.

It's funny that a wife who can see through you doesn't notice a missing button.

It's hard to keep your wife in the dark if you're burning the candle at both ends.

Kissing your own wife is like scratching a place that doesn't itch.

My apartment is antique and so is my wife.

The last time my wife made me a hot meal we had cold cuts.

The only thing my wife can fix around the house are Martinis and Manhattans.

Where there's smoke, there is my wife cooking.

With my wife, food has a way of starting out frozen and ending up burned.

Women

A woman always asks her husband's opinion after she's made up her mind.

A woman can skin a wolf and get a mink.

A woman can stay longer on the phone than on a diet.

A woman doesn't always get the last word. Sometimes she's talking to another woman.

A woman doesn't know which dress she doesn't want until after she buys it.

A woman doesn't mind her husband looking his age as long as he overlooks hers.

A woman dresses for men's eyes and for women's eyebrows.

A woman gets married to make two people happy: herself and her mother.

A woman goes to a football game to look at mink coats.

A woman is a member of the speaker sex.

A woman is a member of the weeper sex.

A woman is a thing of beauty and an expense forever.

A woman is a wife who has heated-up dinners, charged-up bills, a made-up face and a fed-up husband.

A woman is an optimist when she thinks that the man she is about to marry is better than the one she just divorced.

A woman is God's second mistake.

A woman is happy if she has two things: furniture to move around, and a husband to move it around for her.

A woman is never quite so old as her dearest friend says she is.

A woman is only a woman—but a good cigar is a smoke.

A woman is the female of the speeches.

A woman is the so-called tender gender.

A woman never has the last word. She has a million in reserve.

A woman never knows her worst faults until she quarrels with her best friend.

A woman on time is one in nine.

A woman wears a sweater to accentuate the positive and a girdle to eliminate the negative.

A woman who is always harping about something is not necessarily an angel.

A woman who is smart enough to ask a man's advice seldom is dumb enough to take it.

A woman who knows how to dish it out should be able to cook it.

A woman who laughs up her sleeve should marry the man who talks through his hat.

A woman who says all men are alike should marry the man who says he understands women.

A woman who talks all day deserves a husband who snores all night.

A woman's best beauty aid is a nearsighted man.

A woman's dress usually stays in style until the next time she goes shopping.

A woman's vocabulary may be only 500 words, but what a turnover!

All the world is a stage—and the women make most of the scenes.

Any woman who wouldn't mind having a double chin probably has three.

At about forty a woman is old enough to start looking younger.

It takes a woman to make biscuits, but it takes a man to lift them.

It's better for a woman to be two-faced than double-chinned.

It's the woman who pays and pays—with her husband's money.

Many a woman reduce and reduce, but never become bargains.

Many a woman's mistake is covered with a baby blanket.

Marrying a woman for her beauty is like buying a house for its paint.

My new serge suit picks up everything but women.

No woman has ever shot her husband while he was doing the dishes.

Some women are like watches—hard to regulate.

Some women are so hard, only a diamond makes an impression on them.

Some women become blue at the first sign of grey.

Some women don't mind having a man around the house. They just don't want him inside.

Some women even go out and buy a hunting outfit to be dressed correctly when shooting their husbands.

Some women get even with their husbands by staying married to them.

Some women grow old before their time trying to look young after their time.

Some women know their husband's jokes backwards and tell them that way.

Some women show a lot of style and some styles show a lot of women.

Tell a woman a secret and it's no secret anymore.

The better a woman looks, the longer a man does.

The easier a woman is to pick up the harder she is to drop.

The harder a woman tries to look young, the harder it looks like she's trying.

The less there is to a woman's bathing suit the more it cost.

The upkeep of women is the downfall of men.

The woman who can't do anything with her hair could do even less without it.

There are two kinds of women: the kind you dream about and the kind you marry.

When a woman gets a man on the spot she usually takes him to the cleaners.

Women always know everything except why they ever married their husbands.

Women are always ready to forgive and forget. But they will never forget what they forgive.

Women are attractive at twenty, attentive at thirty and adhesive at forty.

Women are entitled to life, liberty and the pursuit of men.

Women are funny. They can't get a hat until they go to town and they can't go to town until they get a hat.

Women are just a rag, a bone and a hank of hair, but what's wrong with the junk business?

Women are just like salads. Much depends on their dressing.

Women are like elephants—Nice to look at, but you wouldn't want to own one.

Women are not what they used to be. They used to be girls.

Women are smarter than men. But did you ever see a man wearing a shirt that buttons down the back?

Women are the best other sex we have.

Women are the kinds of problems men like to wrestle with.

Women are to blame for most of the lying that men do. They insist on asking the questions.

Women are wiser than men because they know less and understand more.

Women's clothes are really crazy. Some wear more when they take a bath than when they walk the street.

Women divide their age by two, double the price of their dresses, triple their husband's salary and add five years to the age of their friends.

Women don't need attics. They have their purses.

Women fall into three groups: looked at, looked over, and overlooked.

Women love the simple things in life: men.

Women make the best wives.

Women only want husbands under their thumb and a roof over their heads.

Women spend 75% of their life sitting down, as the figures clearly show.

Women still remember the first kiss after men have forgotten the last.

Women were made before mirrors and have been before them ever since.

Women were made to be loved, not to be understood.

Women who dress to please men should learn that they don't have to dress to please men.

Women will be the weaker sex as long as they're strong enough to get away with it.

Women will wear anything new no matter how uncomfortable, and men will wear anything comfortable no matter how old.

You usually can tell by a woman's clothing how much she thinks her husband should be making.

5

Clever Quips and Popular Gags

Clever Advice

Don't ...

    ...bite your nails, especially if you are a carpenter.
    ...count your checks before they're cashed.
    ...daydream on the company's time; you might miss the coffee break.
    ...do anything you can't enjoy.
    ...do everything today. Save some mistakes for tomorrow.
    ...drink while driving. You might spill some.
    ...eat your mashed potatoes with your hand. Use a knife!
    ...ever go into the water after a hearty meal; you'll never find it there.
    ...fight a cold. That's what makes a cold sore.
    ...follow your nose, even if it is running.
    ...forget that today is the tomorrow you worried about yesterday.
    ...hang on to your youth—if he's driving.
    ...itch all over. Learn to itch where you can scratch.
    ...itch for something you're not willing to scratch for.
    ...lend people money: it gives them amnesia.
    ...lose your temper—unless you have a bad one.
    ...marry the wrong girl. It's bad enough if you get the right one.
    ...play in the street—you may get that run-down feeling.
    ...remove coffee stains from your suits with a scissor.
    ...speak about your private ailment in public—she might hear you.
    ...spit. Remember the Johnson flood.
    ...sprinkle your lawn when it's raining!
    ...throw kisses unless the girl is a good catch.
    ...work up a head of steam before you find out what's cooking.

Never...

    ...argue with a fool. Onlookers may not know which is which.
    ...break your bread or roll in your soup.
    ...cross a bridge before it is built.
    ...dive into water on an empty stomach. Always do it head first.
    ...drink coffee during the day. It will keep you awake!
    ...drink hot coffee from a saucer.
    ...drink on an empty wallet!
    ...forget a friend—if he owes you anything.
    ...give coffee to a drunk. You'll get a wide-awake drunk.

...go on a hayride with a grass widow.

...hit a child in anger. Wait until you're calm and more accurate.

...hit a man when he's down. He might get up and hit you back.

...insult an alligator until you've crossed the bridge.

...invest your money in anything that eats or needs repairing.

...judge a book by its movie.

...kiss a shoemaker with your eyes closed; he could have a mouthful of nails.

...let a fool kiss you or a kiss fool you.

...let grass grow under your feet. It tickles.

...pet a polar bear until he's a rug.

...play ping-pong with your mouth open.

...put off till tomorrow what you can put off for good.

...put off until tomorrow what you can't shove onto someone else's desk today.

...remove a fly from your wife's forehead with a hammer.

...slap a child in the face. There's a place for everything.

...slap a man while he is chewing tobacco.

...sleep with a mosquito in the room.

...sleep with your eyes open.

...start drinking when you get up in the morning. Get dressed first.

...talk about a butter knife. You know how those things spread.

...tell your troubles to a bartender. It could upset his analyst.

...try to locate a gas leak with a lighted match.

...try to make people feel at home. If they wanted that, they'd have stayed there.

...trouble trouble till trouble troubles you.

The best way to ...

... antique your furniture is to have several children around.

... approach a woman with a past is with a present.

... avoid a car accident is to go by bus.

... avoid a hangover is to keep drinking.

... avoid an automobile accident is to stay home on Sunday.

... avoid alimony is to stay single or stay married.

... avoid having enemies is to outlive them.

... avoid hitting your thumb with a hammer is to hire a carpenter.

... avoid washing the supper dishes is to take your wife out to dinner.

... avoid a nose bleed is to keep out of other people's business.

... avoid old age is to hang yourself.

... avoid trouble is to breathe through your nose. It keeps your mouth shut.

... avoid washing dishes is to have your husband eat out of your hand.

... beat a slot machine is with a sledge hammer.

... better your lot is to do a lot better.

... break a glass is to drop it.

... break a leg is to throw a cigarette down an open manhole and then step on it.

... break an engagement is to marry the girl.

... bring money home from a race track is to be a pickpocket.

... buy a used car is when it's new.

... call a spade a spade is to call a spade a spade.

... camouflage the bow-legs of a woman is with a plunging neckline.

... catch a rabbit is to hide behind a tree and make noise like a carrot.

... change a woman's mind is to agree with her.

... communicate with a fish is to drop him a line.

... cross a street in New York is in a helicopter.

... cure insomnia is to get a lot of sleep.

... cut down on your telephone bill is to let your teenage daughter pay for one.

... cut down on your wife's spending is to hide her credit cards.

... cut your food bill in half is to use a scissors.

... dance the modern way is to tie your shoelaces together and run like hell.

... develop a quick draw is to open a joint account with your wife.

... dig up a date is with a shovel.

... drive a baby buggy is to tickle his feet.

... drive a nail without smashing your fingers is to hold the hammer in both hands.

... drive through a mountain is to use a tunnel.

... eat cream cheese and lox is with a bagel.

... entertain your wife is to listen to her.

... enjoy a motion picture is to send your girl's parents to the movie.

... enjoy a vegetable dinner is to let the cow eat it, and then eat the cow.

... enjoy the summer is by turning the air conditioning on and the TV set off.

... entertain some people is to sit down and listen.

... escape from quicksand is to jump over it.

... fight a woman is with your hat; grab it and run.

... figure out the cost of living is to take your total income and add ten percent.

... fill out a pink slip is with a beautiful body.

... find missing relatives is to get rich.

... find out if talk is cheap is to make a long distance phone call.

... find out if your face is clean, after washing, is to look at your towel.

... find out what a woman thinks of you is to marry her.

... find out what shape the country is in is to look around the beach.

... find out what's really wrong with your old car is to give it to your son for his birthday.

... keep your youth is not to introduce him to anybody.

.. forget all your troubles is to wear a pair of tight shoes.

.. get a charge out of life is with a credit card.

.. get a doctor to make a house call is to marry him.

.. get a good cup of coffee in the morning is to wake your wife first.

.. get a good headache is to have too many drinks the night before.

.. get a hangover is to drink whiskey the night before.

.. get a lot of undivided attention is to make a mistake.

.. get a seat on the bus is to become a bus driver.

.. get a wart off your hand is to marry him.

.. get a woman to drive carefully is to tell her, in case of an accident, the papers will print her true age.

. . . get a woman to keep a secret is to tell her everyone else knows it already.

. . . get a woman to listen is to whisper.

. . . get ahead is to have one.

. . . get ahead in traffic is to leave your car home and walk.

. . . get along with people is to get along with people.

. . . get around your husband is to hug him.

. . . get back on your feet is to get rid of your car.

. . . get into trouble is to be right at the wrong time.

. . . get out of paying taxes for ten years is not to pay them and you will sure get ten years.

. . . get rich is to spend less than you make or make more than you spend.

. . . get rid of a squeak in your car is to leave your wife at home.

. . . get rid of temptation is to yield to it.

. . . get rid of dishpan hands is to let your husband do the dishes.

. . . get rid of party leftovers is to show them the door.

. . . get rid of party leftovers is never to invite them again.

. . . get some people to agree with you is to keep your mouth shut.

. . . get to see a doctor today is to turn on the television set.

. . . get to the top is to get off your bottom.

. . . get up in the world is in an airplane.

. . . get your name in the papers is to walk across the street reading one.

. get your wife to change her mind is to agree with her.

. . . get your wife to go on a diet is to buy her a mink coat three sizes too small.

get your wife's attention is by looking comfortable at a party.

. . . get your wife's attention is to tell her something that's none of her business.

. . . guess a woman's age is not to.

. . . guess a woman's age is without her help.

. . . give up smoking cigarettes is to smoke cigars.

... have a few minutes for herself is for a housewife to start to do the dishes.

... have nine men run after you is to play baseball.

... heat up a chicken is to kiss her.

... hit the bull's eye is to miss everything around it.

... hold a man is in your arms.

... hold liquor is in a glass.

... improve a vegetable dinner is with a big juicy steak.

... improve your appetite is to go on a diet.

... improve your home is to stay out of it.

... keep a family together is to have one car.

... keep a kitchen spotless is not to use it.

... keep a man's love is not to return it.

... keep a skunk from smelling is to cut off his nose.

... keep a thermometer from dropping is to use a strong nail.

... keep apples from spoiling is to place them in a room full of small children.

... keep children's clothes clean for several days is to keep them off the children.

... keep lipstick from smearing is to eat a lot of garlic.

... keep milk from turning sour is to keep it in the cow.

... keep rice from sticking together is to boil each grain separately.

... keep some of your take-home pay is not to go home.

... keep thin is not to exceed the feed limit.

... keep water out of your house is not to pay the water bill.

... keep your daughter out of hot water is to put some dishes in it.

... keep your diet is to shake your head from side to side when offered a second helping.

... keep your dishes clean is to eat out of your pots.

... keep your food bill down is to use a heavier paperweight.

. keep your husband home is to hide the car keys.

... keep your job is to get things mixed up the first day you're on the job so the boss can't fire you.

... keep your teeth in good shape is to mind your own business.

... keep your wife in the kitchen is to put a phone there.

... kill an hour in New York City is to drive around the block.

... kill time is to work.

... learn a woman's true age is to ask her ex-husband.

... learn the value of money is not to have any.

... locate a lost thumbtack is to walk around barefooted.

... look young is to mingle with older people.

... lose a friend is to tell him something for his own good.

... lose control of your car is to forget to make a payment.

... lose weight is to eat only what you don't like.

... lose weight is to keep both your mouth and the refrigerator closed.

... lose weight is to keep within the feed limit.

... lose your shirt is to do business on the cuff.

... make a fire by rubbing two sticks together is to make sure one of them is a match.

... make a monkey out of a man is to ape him.

... make a pile of money is to become a bank teller.

... make a tall man short is to borrow money from him.

... make hamburger taste better is to ask the price of steak.

... make hot tea is to use hot water.

... make money is to forget whom you borrowed from.

... make your eyes pop out is to wear a shirt with too small a collar.

... make your landlord paint the apartment is to move out.

... meet a neighbor is to play your TV set too loud at 2 a.m.

... miss the train is at the crossing.

... preserve life is to stay out of jams.

... preserve the wedding ring is to dip it in hot dishwater twice a day.

... preserve your wool bikini through the winter is to wrap it around a mothball.

... put a fire out is not to have one.

... put your wife in good humor is to wipe the dishes for her.

... raise cabbage is with a knife and fork.

... recapture your youth is to take the car away from him.

... reduce is never to eat while your wife is talking.

... reduce is to set the bathroom scale in front of the refrigerator.

... remain poor is to pretend to be rich.

... remember something is to try and forget it.

... remember your wife's birthday is to forget it once.

... remove coffee stains from a silk dress is with a pair of scissors.

... save a marriage from a divorce is not to show up for the wedding.

... save daylight is to use it.

... save face is to button your lips.

... save face is to keep the lower half shut.

... save face is to stop shooting it off.

... save money is not to spend it.

... save money is to make more than you spend.

... save money nowadays is to have few pockets and short arms.

... save money on your honeymoon is to go alone.

... say goodbye to a man is with a permanent wave.

... see a flying saucer is to pinch the waitress.

... serve leftovers is to someone else.

... settle a strike is to strike a settlement.

... settle my wife's hash is with two spoonfuls of bicarbonate.

... solve the parking problem for the new motorist is to buy a parked car.

... spade the garden is right after your wife tells you to.

... stamp out a hotfoot is to step into a puddle.

... start a day is to stay in bed.

... start to economize is before you run out of money.

... stay awake during after-dinner speeches is to deliver them.

... stay healthy is to eat what you don't like, drink what you don't want, and do what you'd rather not.

... stay in good health is not to get sick.

... stay out of the army is to join the navy.

... stop a bad habit is never to start it.

... stop a runaway horse is to bet on it.

... stop a woman from talking is to kiss her.

... stop hitting your thumb is to have your wife hold the nail.

... stop smoking is to carry wet matches.

... stop smoking is to marry a girl who objects to it.

... stop that noise in your car is to let her take the wheel.

... stop the butler from peeking through the keyhole is to leave the door open.

... stop your wife from spending too much money on gloves is to buy her a new diamond ring.

... support a wife these days is to send her off to work.

... surprise your wife on your anniversary is to mention it.

... talk to a lion is by long distance.

... tell a woman's age is in a whisper.

... tell a woman's age is when she's not around.

... tell if a girl is ripe for love is to squeeze her.

... tell if a modern painting is completed is to touch it. If it's dry, it's finished.

... tell time by the sun is to shade your eyes and look at your watch.

... tell whether a tree is male or female is to look at the limbs.

... test your airbrakes is to drive your car over a cliff.

... tolerate a neighbor's noise is to join the party.

... turn a woman's head is to tell her she has a nice profile.

... watch calories is from a distance.

... wear a sack suit is to take the potatoes out first.

People who live in glass houses ...

... don't do much living.

... had better draw their drapes.

... have as much privacy as a golfish.

... have faded furniture.

... have very little love life.

... look like goldfishes.

... make interesting neighbors.

... might as well answer the doorbell.

... must be nuts!

... should dress in the basement.

... should have chatter-proof neighbors.

... should never get stoned.

... should not undress in the daytime.

... should pull down the blinds.

... should sell flowers.

... should sleep in the basement.

... should take their baths in the dark.

... should use their neighbors' bathroom.

... should wear pajamas at night time.

... shouldn't buy wallpaper.

... shouldn't hit the ceiling.

... shouldn't laugh at fishbowls.

... shouldn't make love near the windows.

... shouldn't play ball.

... shouldn't throw boomerangs.

... shouldn't throw stones.

They now have a doll called ...

... the Abe Lincoln doll—you wind it and it goes straight to the theater.

... the Airplane doll—you wind it and it goes up in the air.

... the Ant doll—you wind it and it goes to a picnic.

... the Astronaut doll—you wind it and it litters the moon.

... the Athlete doll—you wind it and it sticks out its chest.

... the Banana doll—you wind it and it starts peeling.

... the Baseball doll—you wind it and it runs around.

... the Bellhop doll—you wind it and it waits to be tipped.

... the Boomerang doll—you wind it and it always comes back to you.

... the Bowling doll—you wind it and it starts rolling.

... the Boxing doll—you wind it and it hits you in the eye.

... the Boy doll—you wind it and it runs after a girl doll.

... the Bricklayer doll—you wind it and it moves very slowly.

... the Burlesque doll—you wind it and it takes off.

... the Bus Driver doll—you wind it and it stops at every corner.

... the Caddy doll—you wind it and it gets teed off.

... the Car doll—you wind it and it stalls.

... the Carousel doll—you wind it and it goes round and round.

... the Checker doll—you wind it and it starts jumping.

... the Chicken doll—you wind it and it turns yellow.

... the Cigar doll—you wind it and it starts smoking.

... the Cinderella doll—you wind it and it stays out past midnight.

... the Cockroach doll—you wind it and it runs under the kitchen sink.

... the Cold doll—you wind it and it starts sneezing.

... the Cook doll—you wind it and it burns your dinner.

... the Dentist doll—you wind it and it opens its mouth.

... the Dentist doll—you wind it and it starts drilling.

... the Diaper doll—you wind it and it's time for a change.

... the Doctor doll—you wind it and it operates on batteries.

... the Dum-Dum doll—you wind it and it just sits there.

... the Ex-President doll—you wind it and it writes memoirs.

... the Executive doll—you wind it and it gets an ulcer.

... the Executive doll—you wind it and it goes for lunch.

... the Fever doll—you wind it and it runs a temperature.

... the Football doll—you wind it and it starts kicking.

... the Girl Scouts doll—you wind it and it starts selling cookies.

... the Gossip doll—you wind it and it starts to run somebody down.

... the Hangover doll—you wind it and it gives you a headache.

... the Headwaiter doll—you wind it and it looks the other way.

... the Hippie doll—you wind it and it drops out.

... the Hippie doll—you wind it and it needs a cleaning.

... the Hippie doll—you wind it and wind it but it never works.

... the Hippie doll—you wind it and it runs away from home.

... the Hippie doll—you wind it and it runs somebody down.

... the Inflation doll—you wind it up and up and up.

... the Investor doll—you wind it and it yells: Sell!

... the Japanese doll—you wind it and it falls apart.

... the Kangaroo doll—you wind it and it jumps up and down.

... the Kite doll—you wind it and it flies away.

... the Librarian doll—you wind it and she says, "Shhh!"

... the Magician doll—you wind it and it disappears.

... the Magnet doll—you wind it and can't let go of it.

... the Mother-in-law doll—you wind it and it starts nagging.

... the Necklace doll—you wind it and it clings to your neck.

... the Neighbor doll—you wind it and it uses your tools.

... the Old Maid doll—you wind it and it looks under the bed.

... the Old Soldier doll—you wind it and it fades away.

... the Onion doll—you wind it and it makes you cry.

... the Picnic doll—you wind it and it starts to rain.

... the Plumber doll—you wind it and you won't see it for a week.

... the Politician doll—you wind it and it gives you an argument.

... the Poison doll—you wind it and it kills you.

... the Pollution doll—you wind it and it starts gasping for air.

... the Preacher doll—you wind it and it takes up a collection.

... the President doll—you wind it and for four years it does nothing.

... the Psychiatrist doll—you wind it and it lies down on the couch.

... the Reducing doll—you wind it and it disappears.

... the Rip Van Winkle doll—you wind it and it goes to sleep.

... the Secretary doll—you wind it and it jumps on your lap.

... the Secretary doll—you wind it and it's late for work.

... the Senator doll—you wind it and it talks out of both sides of its mouth.

... the Sleeping doll—you wind it and it wakes up.

... the Spring doll—you wind it and it starts busting out all over.

... the Stock Market doll—you wind it and it drops to the bottom.

... the Subway doll—you wind it and it breaks down.

... the Sweetheart doll—you wind it and it says, "I love you!"

... the Taxpayer doll—you wind it and it wrings its hands.

... the Taxi driver doll—you wind it and it dissolves in the rain.

... the Teenager doll—you wind it and it talks on the phone for hours.

... the Telephone doll—you wind it and you get a wrong number.

... the TV doll—you wind it and it starts to flip up and down.

... the Union doll—you wind it and it goes on strike.

... the Voter's doll—you wind it and it moves to the right.

... the Wallpaper doll—you wind it and it creeps up the wall.

... the Welfare doll—you wind it and it stops working.

... the Wet doll—you wind it and you wish you hadn't.

... the Wife doll—you wind it and it runs back home to mother.

... the Wild sea doll—you wind it and it waves.

... the Woman Driver doll—you wind it and it runs down everything.

Every time ...

... I am in a hurry my car won't start.

... I am in a rush my shoelaces break.

... I am in the bathtub my phone rings.

... I answer a phone the call isn't for me.

... I ask for a surprise dinner, my wife takes all the labels off the cans.

... I ask her to take a bath she says, "No soap!"

... I ask my wife for a stiff drink she puts some starch in my highball.

... I ask someone what time it is I get a different answer.

... I buy a suit with two pairs of pants, I burn a hole in the jacket.

... I buy an orange I get a lemon.

... I buy my wife a present she gets so excited she can hardly wait to exchange it.

... I came home from school, my parents had moved.

.. I come home late, my wife and the roast are doing a slow burn.

... I come home late my wife wants to know where I have been before she tells me where to go.

... I come home with my mind made up to stay home, my wife has her mind made up to go out.

... I come to town they give me a party—a going-away party.

... I come up with a fresh idea my secretary slaps me.

... I complain about the TV dinner, my wife blames it on our antenna.

... I dance with a grass widow I get hay fever.

... I dial a number I get a busy signal.

... I dial I get a wrong number.

... I drop a dime it's my last one.

... I eat alphabet soup I only find one letter in it.

... I find a parking meter I have no dime.

... I find a taxi it's off duty.

... I get on a bus it's going the wrong way.

... I get on a ferry it makes me cross.

... I go to a class reunion, I find my classmates are so stout and bald they hardly recognize me.

... I go to a zoo, I have to buy two tickets—one to get in and one to get out.

... I go to the beach it rains.

... I go to the race track I lose my shirt.

... I have a light lunch my wife serves a dark dinner.

... I have dinner in a Chinese place I find the address of a doctor in my fortune cookie.

... I have my car in the middle of a carwash, my autophone starts ringing.

... I have some ideas I have no pencil.

... I kiss my secretary my wife walks in.

... I lend my friend a book he keeps it. He's a professional bookkeeper.

... I look at my wife, I'm sorry I learned how to whistle.

. . . I look at my wife I lose my appetite.

. . . I look at my girl time stands still.

. . . I meet a nice girl, either she's married or I am.

. . . I open a fortune cookie I find a note from my wife to come home at once.

. . . I open my mouth my teeth fall out.

. . . I open my mouth my wife interrupts.

. . . I paper our rooms I can't find the windows.

. . . I play Bingo I get cards without numbers.

. . . I pull a door the sign says: Push.

. . . I put a seashell to my ear I get a busy signal.

. . . I put my foot down my wife steps on it.

. . . I put my watch on my wrist it stops ticking.

. . I reach the station I miss the train.

. . I read a book some pages are missing.

. . I see a four-poster bed I figure it's a lot of bunk.

. . I start my car it stalls.

. . I take a bath my phone rings. After I complained to the phone company, they took away my bathtub.

. . I take a trip I forget something. Last time I forgot my wife.

. . I take a special trip, it's cancelled.

. . I take my wife to a restaurant she eats her head off. And she looks better that way.

. . I think how much aspirin costs, I get a headache.

. . I throw a boomerang away it never comes back.

. . I try to carry a tune I drop it.

. . I try to hit a nail I hit my thumb.

. . I try to sleep my neighbor plays the drum.

. . I turn on the radio I blow a tube.

... I turn over a new leaf, it's poision ivy.

... I use my car I get a flat.

... I want my wife she's out shopping.

... I want to mail a letter I have no stamp.

... I want to make an outside phone call I have no dime.

... I want to park my car I can't find a parking place.

... I want to smoke I have no matches.

... I wash my car it rains.

... I wear my spring coat the springs get rusty in the rain.

... I wind my watch I break the main spring.

... it rains I have no umbrella.

... it rains soup I have only a fork in my hand.

... my car passes a junkyard it gets homesick.

... my girl wears a red dress, she looks like a bow-legged fire engine.

... my girl wears something light, she sure has a heavy date.

... my girl wears that dress, she shows everything but her appetite.

... my horse runs, they have to photograph the track to find him.

... my ship comes in, there's a dock strike.

Every time my wife ...

... answers the phone it's a wrong number.

... brings home a new dress, I tell her to return it in good health.

... buys some doughnuts, she takes the dough and I get the nuts.

... cooks, she burns everything but the cookbook.

... cooks spring chickens, I get the spring and she takes the chicken.

... eats you can see sparks fly from her fork and knife.

... finds a blonde hair on my coat, she sees red.

... goes shopping she comes home with everything but money.

... goes to an antique show someone tries to buy her.

... has an accident in the kitchen I get it for dinner.

... is in the bathtub they want her on the phone.

... looks at my head she puts melon on her shopping list.

... puts a fire cracker on my chair, I blow my top.

... sees an empty parking space she asks me to buy a car.

... serves alphabet soup the letters spell out *poison.*

... serves health food I get sick.

... serves me a square meal it doesn't fit in my round stomach.

... serves me home-made jello I get a lump in my throat.

... tries out a new recipe from her mother I get a new prescription from my doctor.

... washes an ice cube in hot water she can't find it.

The honeymoon is over ...

... when baby talk comes from the nursery.

... when bushels of kisses become infrequent pecks.

... when he doesn't notice she bought something new until he gets the bill.

... when he finds out he married a big spender and she finds out she didn't.

... when he gets out of the car in a drive-in movie to wipe the windshield.

... when he has to wash and iron his own apron.

... when he orders a hamburger with plenty of onions.

... when he prefers to stay out instead of in.

... when he starts to wheeze instead of squeeze.

... when he starts wishing he'd married a good cooker instead of a good looker.

... when he stays out all night and she doesn't even know it.

... when he stops praising her clothes and starts pricing them.

... when he takes her off the pedestal and puts her on a budget.

... when he takes off his toupee around the house.

. . . when she burns the dinner and he burns up.

. . . when she gets flabby, gabby and crabby.

. . . when she gives him a hot tongue and a cold shoulder.

. . . when she starts calling him "Listen" instead of "Honey."

. . . when she starts complaining about the noise he makes preparing breakfast.

. . . when she stops crying on his shoulder and starts jumping on his neck.

. . . when she stops dropping her eyes and starts raising her voice.

. . . when she stops helping you with the dishes.

. . . when she wants something else around her neck besides your arms.

when the billing exceeds the cooing.

. . when the kiss that was a temptation becomes an obligation.

. . . when the mother-in-law walks in with her own key.

. . . when they decide to convert the love seat into two TV chairs.

. . . when warm hearts become hot heads.

. . . when you no longer drink to her, but because of her.

. . . when you would rather see the kitchen in good shape than a good shape in the kitchen.

. . . when your dog brings your slippers and your wife barks at you.

If

If a girl doesn't marry the man she wants, pity the man she gets.

If a girl doesn't watch her figure, the boys won't either.

If a girl has a nice stairway she doesn't need much upstairs.

If a girl is good there's no need to be careful; and if she's careful, there's no need for her to be good.

If a girl is treated like a hot-house flower, she'll come home potted.

If a girl wants to be seen in the best places, she should wear a lowcut gown.

If a girl wears a new dress, women want to know where she got it; if she wears a new mink, they want to know *how* she got it.

If a man bites a dog, he is probably eating a frankfurter.

If a man is too lazy to think for himself, he should get married.

If a man wants his dream to come true, he must wake up.

If at first you don't succeed...

    ...a lot of people will tell you why.
    ...call up another girl.
    ...cheat!
    ...cheer up—you'll get used to the pattern.
    ...deduct the loss.
    ...try again when nobody is watching.
    ...try borrowing from somebody else.
    ...try doing it the way your wife told you.
    ...try looking in the wastebasket for directions.
    ...try reading the instructions.
    ...try, try again or get somebody else to do it.
    ...you probably haven't accomplished much.
    ...you're fired.
    ...you're like most other people.
    ...you're not related to the boss.
    ...you're running about average.

If both of your shoes feel uncomfortable, maybe you've got them on the wrong feet!

If everything is coming your way, you're probably in the wrong lane.

If God had meant us to fly he would have given us propellers on our shoulders.

If George Washington was alive today, he'd be most noted for his old age.

If her dress were any shorter it would be a belt.

If life hands you a lemon, squeeze it hard and start a lemonade stand.

If looks could kill, a lot of people would die with their bridge cards in their hands.

If love is blind, marriage must be an eye-opener.

If my car were a horse it would be shot.

If my girl said what she thought, she'd be speechless.

If my wife doesn't show up in three days in a row at Saks Fifth Ave., they send her a get-well card.

If my wife doesn't stop nagging me, I'll let my insurance lapse.

If my wife keeps buying colonial furniture, there's going to be an American revolution in my house.

If my wife didn't keep a budget we wouldn't know how much we owe.

If I was in this business for the business, I wouldn't be in business.

If I were a calendar, I'd have lots of dates.

If I were a clock, I'd never strike!

If I were a telephone I wouldn't ring when there's nobody home.

If I were eight feet tall, I'd be a giant.

If I were in your shoes, I'd get a shine.

If it hadn't been for that fellow Edison, we'd watch TV by candlelight.

If it is hard to dust, it's probably antique.

If it wasn't for marriage, husbands and wives would have to fight with strangers.

If it weren't for airplane schedules we would never know how late the planes are.

If it weren't for my wife, I wouldn't be what I am today: broke!

If it weren't for the step-on garbage can, many a husband would never get a chance to put his foot down.

If only I had been born rich instead of so darned lovable!

If postal rates go up again we may have a rates riot.

If prosperity can get this country into the mess it's in, just think what a depression could do.

If that dress was cut any lower, she'd be barefoot!

If the cost of living gets any higher, the only thing you can save for a rainy day will be an umbrella.

If the shoe fits, it's out of style.

If the stock market drops any lower, I'll store my certificates in the basement.

If they would freeze food right after it's cooked, you could defrost it when you need it and it would still be hot.

If they would serve my wife's cooking in prison, there would be a riot.

If this is coffee, bring me some tea; but if this is tea, bring me some coffee.

If things ever get back to normal, we'll probably wonder what's wrong.

If two women wearing the same hat smile at each other, they're twins.

If we get just one more deduction on our take-home pay, we won't have a home to take the pay to.

If you are driving make sure you have a car.

If you are fishing for compliments you have to get some better bait.

If you are going to hate yourself in the morning, sleep until noon.

If you are late for work, don't tell your boss.

If you are not afraid to face the music you may lead a band some day.

If you are not confused, you are not well informed.

If you're not too busy for the next hour, I'd like to talk to you for a minute

If you're offered the world on a silver platter, take the platter.

If you are shot out of a cannon the best way to land is on your back.

If you are the ladder to paradise, let me climb into your heart.

If you can eat the right food all the time, you'll die healthy.

If you can guess how many candies I have, I'll give you both of them.

If you can tell the difference between good advice and bad advice, you don't need advice.

If you can't be good, be careful.

If you can't be satisfied with what you receive, be thankful for what you escaped.

If you can't beat them join them.

If you can't brush after every meal, comb!

If you can't find it in the dictionary, the atlas, or the encyclopedia, don't be discouraged; ask for it in the drugstore.

If you can't find the girl of your dreams, marry somebody else meanwhile.

If you can't get a lawyer who knows the law, get one who knows the judge.

If you can't keep your head above water, get a job in a submarine.

If you can't love your enemies, compromise: forget them!

If you can't make a girl melt in your arms, maybe you're not so hot.

If you can't understand it—oppose it!

If you cheat on a diet you gain in the end.

If you chew tobacco don't spit against the wind!

If you do housework for $50 a week, that's domestic. If you do it for nothing, that's matrimony.

If you don't crack the egg you can't beat it.

If you don't do it, you'll never know what would have happened if you *had* done it.

If you don't enjoy it, don't do it.

If you don't go away and leave me alone, I'll find someone who will.

If you don't hear a pin drop, then something is wrong with your bowling.

If you don't know what's up, you haven't been shopping lately.

If you don't like her cooking, keep your mouth shut.

If you don't like the way a woman drives, get off the sidewalk.

If you don't like your neighbor, buy each of his children a drum.

If you don't pay alimony in due time, you do time.

If you don't use soap, be sure and use some perfume!

If you don't worry about your diet everything may go to pot.

If you drink beer for 1,000 months, you'll live to be a hundred.

If you drink like a fish—don't drive like a maniac.

If you drink like a fish, don't drive—swim!

If you eat vegetables for 80 years you won't die young.

If you expect less from me, you'll get just what you expect.

If you fall in love make sure it's someone you like.

If you find yourself in hot water, be nonchalant: take a bath.

If you give up wearing glasses you'll look better, but you won't see as well.

If you have a headache thrust your head through a window and the pane will disappear.

If you have a minute to spare, tell me all you know.

If you have half a mind to get married, do it. That's all it takes.

If you have water on the knee, hand the baby back to mother.

If you haven't a leg to stand on, it's smarter not to kick.

If you keep your nose to the grindstone you're bound to lose face.

If you knew Susi like I know Susi, you'd take out Gertrude.

If you lend a friend five dollars and never see him again, it was worth it.

If you let a smile be your umbrella, you'll be the happiest drenched person in the world.

If you let a smile be your umbrella, you'll get a mouthful of rain.

If you like me, smile!

If you like your suit, keep wearing it—no matter what people say.

If you look like your passport photo, an extra week of vacation may help   .

If you married her for her money you sure got cheated.

If you missed your train, the best thing to do is wait for the next one.

If you reach the opera before it is finished, you're still on time.

If you really want to learn a woman's age, ask somebody who hates her.

If you see a person without a smile, give him one of yours.

If you see the handwriting on the wall, there's a child in the family.

If you sleep like a baby at night you don't have one.

If you spit against the wind, you get it in the face.

If you squeeze the wrong doll in a toystore, she'll yell for the manager.

If you tell the truth you don't have to remember everything.

If you think marriage is a 50:50 proposition, you've flunked your course in fractions.

If you think practice makes perfect, you don't have a child taking piano lessons.

If you think she's beautiful, you should see her photographs.

If you think the boss never laughs, ask him for a raise.

If you think time heals everything, try sitting it out in a doctor's office.

If you think you have no problems, you have problems.

If you think you work harder than the average worker, then you're an average worker.

If you want an endless summer don't send your kids to summer camp.

If you want my opinion, you've got superb taste.

If you want to avoid dishpan hands, wash the dishes with your feet.

If you want to avoid that run-down feeling—stay home.

If you want to be a stand-out beauty, mingle with ugly people.

If you want to be different these days—just act normal.

If you want to drive your wife nuts, smile in your sleep.

If you want to forget all your troubles, wear tight shoes.

If you want to get your troubles off your mind, go horseback riding.

If you want to have the last word with your wife, just say: I apologize!

If you want to see a cricket match you have to buy a cricket ticket.

If you want to sit and watch the world go by, buy a cheap, used car.

If you want something to get for your money, buy a wallet.

If you want to know how old a woman is, ask her sister-in-law.

If you want to lose your blues, send them parcel post.

If you want to make money last, you've got to make it first.

If you want to see a baseball game in the worst way, take your wife along.

If you want to see something swell, just hit your head with a baseball bat.

If you want to write something that will live forever, sign a mortgage.

If you want your money to last longer, charge things to other people.

If you want your wife to leave, eat crackers in bed all night.

If you want your wife to listen, talk to another woman.

If you watch a game it's fun; if you play it, it's recreation; if you work at it, it's golf.

If you were the only girl in the world, with my luck you'd be my sister.

If you wish to broaden your mind, place a stick of dynamite in each ear and put your head in the barbecue.

If you wonder what your wife does with all the grocery money, stand sideways and look in the mirror.

If you wonder where your child left the roller skates, try walking around the house in the dark.

If your breaks don't work, try to run into something cheap.

If your child wants to lick the beaters on the mixer, make sure to shut it off before letting him.

If your nose smells and your feet run, you're built upside down.

If your ship comes in, you can be assured relatives will be waiting.

If your wife doesn't treat you like she should, be grateful.

If your wife isn't talking to you, don't interrupt.

If your wife laughs at your jokes, it means either that you have a good joke or a good wife.

If your wife wants to learn how to drive, don't stand in her way.

If women talked only about what they understood, the silence would be unbearable.

Useless Information

A bird in your hand is useless if you want to blow your nose.

A horseshoe will never fit a rabbit foot.

A piece of bread held in your mouth will prevent whistling.

Alaska is a state where you think of Canada as the tropics.

Alaska is great if you happen to be a polar bear.

All streets in New York City run parallel to the ground.

As a child, so they tell me, I was very young.

Before knocking on wood see if the doorbell works.

Eating on an empty stomach is apt to be followed by loss of appetite.

Extinct birds lay very few eggs.

It is illegal to keep a horse in a bathtub.

It is proven that since they put the dictionary in alphabetical order, it is much easier to find words.

It is silly to make predictions, especially about the future.

More water is used for making oceans than anything else.

No matter how you move it, writing paper remains stationary.

No matter how you turn it, an upside down cake is always upside down.

Planting stringbeans in damp, warm asphalt is a waste of time.

Rubbing hair restorer into your head will give you very hairy fingertips.

Spots may be removed from rugs by taking a razor blade and cutting around the spot.

The reason an elephant drinks so much water is because nobody offers him anything else.

The speed of lightning would be faster if it didn't stop for the zig-zags.

There are twice as many feet in the world as there are people.

To keep a thermometer from falling use a stronger nail.

To make an omelet you must have some eggs.

Venetian blinds have a shady reputation.

You can't fall out of bed if you sleep on the floor.

You can't milk a cow with a monkey wrench.

The Loser

All he ever gets is warm beer and cold women.

All he ever gets on a silver platter is tarnish.

All his junk mail comes postage due.

Aspirin gives him a headache.

Even if he played bingo alone he wouldn't win.

He bought some handkerchiefs and they were the wrong size.

He bought some horseradish and asked for the horse.

He bought some stock at 12 and it went down 15 points.

He calls for the right time and gets a wrong answer.

He calls for the weather report and the computer hangs up on him.

He got a blow-out in his spare tire in his car trunk.

He keeps one foot in the grave and the other on a banana peel.

He had the 24-hour virus for three weeks.

He has done so much with so little for so long that now he can't do anything with anything anymore.

He got some homing pigeons that don't.

He hung up his stockings last Christmas and all he found was a note from the Health Department.

He is a poor loser, but have you ever seen a rich one?

He is not a good loser; in fact, that's all he ever does.

He went ice fishing and caught 2,000 pounds of ice.

Health food makes him sick.

His artificial flower died.

His fire-proof safe burned down.

His goldfish forgot how to swim.

His goldfish got seasick.

His goldfish looks like him.

His gold watch turned green.

His heating pad doesn't get warm.

His 100-year-old turtle died.

His lifetime pen broke.

His safe deposit box at the bank is missing.

His swimming pool burned down.

His sundial is slow.

His thermo-bottle is leaking.

His toupee is getting bald.

His watchdog was stolen.

His water-proof basement is flooded.

If his ship ever comes in, it will be the Titanic.

Some families have family trees; he has a family bush.

The only break he ever got was a coffee break.

The only break he ever got was in his leg.

The only thing he ever got free was fresh air.

When he carried his young bride over the threshold he got a hernia.

When he found a pair of shoes they were two left ones.

When he got a divorce the judge gave him custody of his wife's parents.

When he was born the doctor picked him up the wrong way and slapped his face.

When his garbage was stolen the police returned it in five days.

Tricky Questions

Can a lover be called a suitor when he doesn't suit her?

Can a man be arrested for striking a match?

Can you beat the drum of your ear?

Can you sit in the shade of the palm of your hand?

Did you ever have the measles, and if so, how many?

Did you ever take off a take-off?

Did you know that a pinch of salt tastes much better if you drop it in a glass of beer?

Did you see in the newspaper that all people die in alphabetical order?

Do people in water beds sleep in life jackets?

Do they have coffee breaks at tea companies?

Do you call a plumber's assistant a drainee?

Do you have to wear a tea-shirt while serving tea?

Do you know why days break and nights fall?

Does it hurt to crack a joke?

How can you sharpen shoulder blades?

How can you travel into the four corners of the world if the world is round?

How come black cows eat green grass and give white milk?

How does Daylight Savings work? Do you move your clock up or down?

How is it possible for a two-pound box of candy to make you gain five pounds?

How many loops in a loophole?

How many peas in a peanut?

How much butter is in a buttercup?

How much does a poundcake weigh?

How much does the milky way?

How much is a Kennel-worth?

How much sand is in a sandwich?

How much Scotch is in Scotch Tape?

If a baker works in a bakery where does a butcher work?

If a beefsteak is tough, is a bar-tender?

If a biscuit is a soda cracker, is an ice pick a water cracker?

If a boat should sink would a safety razor?

If a brewer works in a brewery, who works in a factory?

If a bride wears white for happiness why does the groom wear black?

If a broker is broke does a sewer sew?

If a cook gets his pay, what does a coffee urn?

If a cropduster is cropdusting is a hitchhiker hitchhiking?

If a draft passes through a bank, does it give the clerks a cold?

If a drummer will drum, will a geyser geys?

If a duck can swim, can a spar-row?

If a fellow gets a divorce from a liberated woman, is it a dis-Ms-al?

If a fiddle is wood, is a trom-bone?

If a fishnet catches fish, does a hairnet catch hair?

If a fortification is a large fort, is a ratification a large rat?

If a hatband is a band on a hat, is a husband a band on a hus?

If a horse nibbles grass, can a cat nip tea?

If a jeweler works in a jewelry store, does a nurse work in a nursery?

If a man born in Poland is a Pole, is a man born in Holland a Hole?

If a man doesn't like his aunt, is he anti-aunty?

If a man eats dates, is he consuming time?

If a man from Great Neck is a Great Necker, and a man from Baltimore is a Batimoron, is a man from Cincinnati a Cincinut?

If a man is a pa, is a Pan a ma?

If a meat market sells meat, what do you buy at a fleamarket?

If a milkman sells milk, what does a garbage man sell?

If a painter paints, does a waiter wait?

If a pickpocket picks pockets, why isn't he called a pocketpicker?

If a plyer plyes does a customer custom?

If a pressure cooker cooks pressure, does a meat loaf?

If a printer prints does a stationer make a station?

If a rose fades, does a shirt waist?

If a rubber band stretches, will a bed spread?

If a snowball is made from snow, what are snow tires made of?

If a weightlifter lifts weight, does a shoplifter lift shops?

If a young child is a baby, is a young doctor a baby doctor?

If all brides are so beautiful, where do all those ugly women come from?

If big elephants have big trunks, do little elephants have suitcases?

If Christmas comes, can bills be far behind?

If coyful is full of coy, is bashful full of bash?

If dogfood is food for dogs, is chicken soup for chickens?

If I don't pay alimony this month, can my wife repossess me?

If I ever find the girl of my dreams, what will I do with my wife?

If I ever told you you have a beautiful body, would you hold it against me?

If ignorance is bliss, why aren't more people happy?

If it is a small world, why does it cost so much to run it?

If it takes an apple a day to keep the doctor away, what does it take to get rid of the nurse?

If life is just a bowl of cherries, why do I get all the pits?

If money doesn't grow on trees, why do banks have so many branches?

If olive oil comes from olives, where does baby oil come from?

If owls are so smart, how come they can't get off the night shift?

If Pearl Street is crooked, is Union Square?

If rain makes grass grow, why does it rain on the sidewalk?

If the moon has a baby, will the sky rock-et?

If the Statue of Liberty was shaking, would an ocean liner?

If the world is getting smaller, how come it takes me longer to go to work?

If the world is getting smaller, why do they raise the postal rates?

If there is a woman for every man, how come I got you?

If they would build a temple in Shirley, Long Island, would they call it Shirley Temple?

If we get honey from honeybees do we get butter from butterflies?

If you are so smart, why aren't you rich?

If you eat a TV dinner in front of your radio, can you put your tea cup on a coffee table?

If you feed sheep ironized yeast will you get steel wool?

If you fill your water bed with beer, would you get a foam mattress?

If you get hurt crossing on the Green, will the Red Cross pay for the Blue Cross?

If you order a manhattan in Pittsburgh, can you order a Pittsburgh in Manhattan?

If you should get kicked by a cow, would you call it a milk punch?

If you stop your watch will you save time?

If your mother sits on the front steps is she a step-mother?

If your nose stops up tonight, how will you smell tomorrow?

Is a fireplace a place where you get fired?

Is a piggy bank a bank for piggies?

Is a lover of liver a liver lover?

To be or not to be, that's the question; but what is the answer?

Say, are you reading the paper you are sitting on?

What does a wet martini taste like?

What do you send a sick florist?

What ever became of Whistler's father?

What good is happiness? Can it buy money?

What kinds of pictures have you been taking that you have to develop them in the dark?

What will happen to Scotland Yard when we go metric?

When people ask me what I see in you, what should I tell them?

Where can you buy a cap for your knee?

Where can you get a key to the lock of your hair?

Where does a nudist put his key after he locks his car?

Where does the sun go when she goes down?

Where does your lap go when you get up?

Where does weight go when you lose it?

Who burnt Sienna?

Who tells a bus driver where to get off?

Who travels the bridge of your nose?

Whose uncle is Uncle Sam?

Why are there so many holes in Swiss Cheese when it's the Limburger that needs the ventilation?

Why does a cranky TV set always work perfectly during the commercials?

Why does it take four weeks' salary to pay for a two-week vacation?

Why don't you call a flying fish a swimming bird?

Why don't you call a swimming instructor a hold-up man?

Why is it every time my arms are filled with packages the sign on the door says *Pull?*

Why is it that people who say, "It goes without saying" never go without saying?

Why is it that the late, late TV show usually features an early, early movie?

Why is it when you tighten one shoe lace it always loosens the other?

Why would a hotel have a television set in a bridal suite?

Show me . . .

. . . a baby porcupine and I'll show you a thorny issue.

. . . a baby with a fever and I'll show you a hotsy-totsy.

. . . a baker who runs out of custard and I'll show you a humble pie.

. . . a bikini and I'll show you a fishing net for catching men.

. . . a burned-out post office and I'll show you a case of blackmail.

. . . a cat that just ate a lemon and I'll show you a sourpuss.

. . . a charging nanny goat and I'll show you a flying buttress.

. . . a clean newspaper and I'll show you a parrot with a problem.

. . . a cross between a fox and a mink and I'll show you a fink.

. . . a cross between a mule and a fox and I'll show you a fool.

. . . a family on a diet and I'll show you a very hungry family.

. . . a famous composer's liquor cabinet and I'll show you Beethoven's Fifth.

. . . a famous surgeon and I'll show you a big operator.

. . . a fowl with an artificial leg and I'll show you a lame duck.

. . . a frog on a lily pad and I'll show you a toadstool.

. . . a gallery and I'll show you a Hall of Frame.

. . . a home where the buffalo roams and the deer and the antelope play and I'll show you a messy house.

. . . a leaky faucet and I'll show you a drip tease.

. . . a luxury and I'll show you something that makes life richer and the buyer poorer.

. . . a magician's notebook and I'll show you a spellbinder.

. . . a monarch who takes tea at four and I'll show you the King's English.

. . . a one-word commercial and I'll show you an adverb.

. . . a pallbearer and I'll show you a man who gives a friend a lift.

... a part-time magician and I'll show you an Abracadabbler.

... a pharaoh who ate crackers in bed and I'll show you a crummy mummy.

... a school teacher and I'll show you a disillusioned woman who used to think she liked children.

... a sewing circle and I'll show you a place where women go to needle each other.

... a singing beetle and I'll show you a humbug.

... a squirrel's nest and I'll show you the Nutcracker Suite.

... a stolen sausage and I'll show you a missing link.

... a surgeon and I'll show you a doctor who knows people inside out.

... a wife and a mother-in-law in the backseat and I'll show you a steering committee.

... a young lad's bed and I'll show you a boycott.

... an arsenist and I'll show you a man with a burning desire.

... an obstetrician and I'll show you a friend of Labor.

.. Eve's perfume and I'll show you an Adam balm.

... the first President's denture and I'll show you the George Washington Bridge.

... two dozen satisfied rabbits and I'll show you 24 carats.

... where Stalin is buried and I'll show you a Communist plot.

Show me a man who ...

... beats his wife and I'll show you a good bridge player.

... builds castles in the air and I'll show you a very stupid architect.

... can eat, drink and be merry and I'll show you a fat, grinning drunk.

... can hold his liquor and I'll show you a man with a serious kidney condition.

... can laugh at himself and I'll show you a man with no entertainment expenses.

... can pay his Christmas bills in January and I'll show you a financial genius.

... doesn't turn to look at a pretty girl and I'll show you a man walking with his wife.

... carries a torch and I'll show you a firebug.

... cleans the apartment and I'll show you a self-maid man.

... does what he wants and I'll show you a bachelor.

... doesn't know the meaning of the word *free* and I'll show you a man who has no dictionary.

... drives to the bank in a snowstorm and I'll show you a man who made the last payment on his mortgage.

... enrolls for a course in ethics and I'll show you a man who's in a class by himself.

... gets down on his hands and knees and I'll show you a man who dropped his contact lenses.

... gets up in the morning to write poetry and I'll show you a man going from bed to verse.

... has four daughters and only one bathroom and I'll show you a dirty old man.

... has a million dollars and I'll show you a rich man.

... has his nose to the grindstone and I'll show you a man with some skin off.

... has kissed the Blarney Stone and I'll show you a man with a sex problem.

... has very little money and I'll show you a bum.

... is a good loser and I'll show you a man who's playing golf with his boss.

... is a harpist and I'll show you a plucky musician.

... is a pickpocket and I'll show you a man who picks pockets.

... is a used-car dealer and I'll show you a man who is a wheeler dealer.

... is afraid of Christmas and I'll show you a Noel Coward.

... is always smiling and I'll show you a man who is proud of his teeth.

... is an eccentric millionaire and I'll show you a fortune cookie.

... is contented and I'll show you a man with a poor memory and no imagination.

... is convicted of two crimes and I'll show you a compound sentence.

. is in hot water and I'll show you a man who doesn't have cold feet.

. is not afraid of his wife and I'll show you a bachelor.

... is seasick and I'll show you a man with ocean-motion notion.

... is stopping on the street to buy a hot dog and I'll show you a man curbing his appetite.

... is under ether and I'll show you a man in an aroma coma.

... keeps his both feet on the ground and I'll show you a man who can't get his pants on.

... likes to be interrupted in the middle of a sentence and I'll show you a man who is tired of being in jail.

... likes to sleep all day and I'll show you a bed bug.

... loves concerts and I'll show you a symphomaniac.

... misses his train and I'll show you a man who is late for work.

... puts his shoulder to the wheel and I'll show you a man with a torn jacket.

... smiles when things go wrong and I'll show you a repairman.

... starts at the top and ends up at the bottom and I'll show you a paperhanger.

... sleeps during a political speech and I'll show you a bulldozer.

... understands women and I'll show you a man who is in for a big surprise.

... walks in the rain and I'll show you a man who is all wet.

... walks with his head held high and I'll show you a man who hasn't quite gotten used to his bifocals.

... walks with his head up and I'll show you a man with a stiff neck.